DIGITAL TSUNAMI

THRIVING IN THE 21ST CENTURY

GREG GUTKOWSKI

ISBN: 978-1981340613

TO MONIKA

Special thanks to Nina Fazio for help with this book.

CONTENTS

i
PREFACE

It you recognize any of these frustrations, this book is for you:

- You marvel at the astonishing rate of technological change but wonder how long you can keep up with it

- You wonder how your job and industry will be impacted by artificial intelligence, automation, and outsourcing

- You feel that teenagers know more about digital technologies than you do

- You wonder how to advise your children or students on the best education and careers of the 21st century

- You sense you need to catch up on digital technologies knowledge but do not know where start

- You are confused by digital media jargon, hype, and mixed messages about the impact of technology on your career, life, local economic development, and society as a whole

1

- You feel you need a common sense explanation of many confusing digital technology terms such as:

  - Artificial Intelligence

  - Internet of Things

  - Augmented and Virtual Reality

  - Blockchain

  - Machine Learning

  - Big Data

  - Data Science/Digital Analytics

  - API

  - Cloud And Mobile Computing

  - Digital Marketing

  - E-commerce

  - Telemedicine

  - Drones

  - Robotics

  - 3D Printing

  - Cyber security

  - Digital privacy

ii
FOREWARD

My dad was a very fortunate man. Born in 1904 to a family that bought the second automobile in Newark, NJ, he lived 95 years to a time when virtually anyone who wanted an automobile could have one. He saw weekly deliveries of ice for his icebox end with the advent of refrigerators and watched first-hand the development of television by a Dumont engineer who lived in an apartment building in which he had ownership. By the time of his death, he was aware of computers but not really sure what they accomplished or why anyone would want one. He would sum up the dramatic changes he had seen in his lifetime by describing how he had walked in front of his family's first car with a lantern in the fog and lived long enough to drive a car with headlights that came on automatically when needed.

Longevity runs in my father's family; his oldest brother died one week short of his 103rd birthday! And now I'm staring down my own 80th birthday later this year. And if my dad thought that the world changed rapidly and dramatically in his lifetime, my eighty years have seen even more accelerated change. The carriage stoop in front of our apartment building is now unnecessary in an age of autonomous self-driving vehicles. Carrying cash also is now unnecessary since the advent of credit cards. Computers and the internet have impacted every aspect of my life for better or for worse, and I can carry my phone virtually anywhere since it's small enough to fit in my pocket. While I relied on maps for the first decades of my driving, my car now knows exactly where it is and often where it is going. It can even locate the nearest gas station in an area where I'm traveling for the very first time. And my car also has its own phone that can call for help automatically if it detects an emergency. The car's many sensors alert me to possible system malfunctions and send me emails that detail what I need to do in response such as add air to the tires or get an oil change. The vehicle that I recently traded warned me of a rear axle problem that could disable the car just before I was about to drive high up into the mountains. Three cheers for the Mahwah,NJ Cadillac dealership whose service department not only was open on a Saturday but who happened to stock this axle part that apparently rarely fails.

What changes can I expect to experience if my own longevity matches that of my dad's? If I believe Greg's ground-breaking book, these digital transformations will be far beyond my comprehension. In fact. I'm challenged to speculate on how human beings will have to evolve in order to live in the digital world he describes in the following pages. So I invite you, the reader, to go with Greg on this remarkable journey; you will be richly rewarded for traveling with him.

Leslie Krieger, Ph.D., SPHR
President / Consulting Psychologist
Assessment Technologies Group

iii
INTRODUCTION

Today, humanity as a whole doubles our knowledge base every year. In the near future we will be doubling it every 12 hours![1] This is happening as digital technologies continue to get cheaper, faster, easier to use, and even more omnipresent. Worldwide, there are already more smartphones than toothbrushes or toilets. Each smartphone has more computing power than the computers that took us to the first Moon landing.

Knowledge is defined here as all the data, text files, audio, videos, and images created by all humans globally. But, defined this way, knowledge does not imply effective use of it all. Knowledge by itself, without translating it into wise action with a new product, application, or service, is just useless digits rusting away on some remote hard drive.

It is very unlikely that we are going to slow the trend toward generating more knowledge. At the same time, the average human IQ and/or capacity to process knowledge is not likely to expand anytime soon. Actually, most of our cerebrums are already showing symptoms of overheating from information overload.
So how do we close this serious gap? How can humans thrive with such constantly expanding amounts of data, information, and knowledge? This is what this book is all about.

We don't have all the answers, but we have a lot of experience dealing with data, information, and knowledge in most industries and companies of all sizes. Over the last 20 years, we have helped numerous Fortune Global 500 as well as mom-and-pop small businesses. This allows us to share our experiences on what has worked in the past in these arenas. It also provides us with a unique perspective to formulate a vision of what may work in the future.

In a nutshell, you have the choice to ride the wave of the digital tsunami or to be swept away by it. To thrive in the 21st century, you will need a good 'digital surfboard' made of a combination of the right skills, aptitudes, and attitudes. The trick will be to develop an ideal combination of individual skills based on individual aptitudes. This will have to be coupled with the right attitude toward lifetime learning as well as cooperation utilizing superior communication skills.

For such a vision to materialize on an individual level, at least three things will have to happen:

- Easy access to easily digestible knowledge about what is out there digitally, presented as instructional, motivational, and inspirational, especially for young students
- Self-assessment of aptitudes in the context of that knowledge
- Subsequent skills development based on such assessment

On a community level, we will have to provide much better matching of educational, professional, employment, and other economic opportunities. Today, most of the matching happens with respect to traditional jobs based on rigid resumes and inflexible job and task descriptions. Future jobs will change faster than current job descriptions are being updated now!

We need to improve this inefficient process and also expand it to support aptitudes, talents, attitudes, apprenticeships, internships, entrepreneurship and continuous education beyond K-12 and college. New digital technologies can be highly relevant here by connecting all members of the community and facilitating seamless matching based on complex multidisciplinary criteria beyond simplistic and rigid job descriptions.

It is worth noting that 70% of the U.S. population has no college degree. This is similar to most developed countries. But even a college degree is not enough for one to thrive in the 21st century. However, the future belongs to individuals who, regardless of their official educational attainment, will treat learning as a key lifetime activity. Such an attitude toward education will allow people to continually reassess their own aptitudes and skills in the context of never-ending change.

For this to happen, we need to create easy access to top quality education that demonstrates the impact of never ending digital transformation on our careers, lives, and society as a whole. Digital technologies can play a great role here providing omni-channel online education to support a variety of learning styles.

Economic progress and development cannot be effectively managed by a central authority. It can be influenced by central tax and regulation policies, but it will not happen without a superior, sustainable, and community-based coordination of local talents, skills, education, and economic opportunities.

---

http://www.industrytap.com/knowledge-doubling-every-12-months-soon-to-be-every-12-hours/3950

PART I
ABOUT THE DIGITAL TRANSFORMATION

1
DIGITAL TRANSFORMATION DEFINED

'The best way to predict the future is to digitize it.'

Today, in your pockets, each of you carries a smartphone with more computing power than was used to send the Apollo mission to the Moon and back.

- The price of computing decreased about 10,000 times in the last 20 years. So the computing power of our smartphone would have cost about $4 million 20 years ago.
- Let's assume that twenty years ago, a nice Corvette cost about $30,000 and it was getting 15 miles per gallon. If we were to use the same 10,000 ratio of price decrease, a nice Corvette would cost us 3 dollars today and we would be getting 150,000 miles per gallon.
- As of 2016, more people around the world own smartphones than toothbrushes or toilets.
- The number of active worldwide users on Facebook exceeds the total population of the United States by a factor of 4—about 1.6 billion compared to about 320 million.
- Five technology companies —Apple, Google, Microsoft, Amazon, and Facebook—are among the top 10 largest companies in the U.S.

These metrics depict the breakneck nature of the digital revolution. In a nutshell, we are witnessing an unprecedented development in the history of humankind. Never have we experienced such a rapid increase in the power of technology with a simultaneously steep drop in pricing. These two drivers account for most of the progress and disruption.

Moore's Law

Gordon Moore, the Co-founder of Intel, predicted in 1965 that the capabilities of computing power would double every two years with no increase in price. He was right, and most experts, including Moore himself, expect this law to hold for at least another two decades. Thus, we can expect a similar rate of technological change for another 20 years!

There has been a corresponding decrease in the cost of telecommunications. It would have been unthinkable 20 years ago to watch Netflix movies on a Wi-Fi connected tablet at home. The networks would be way too slow, and the cost would be completely prohibitive.

The Impact

Today, digital technologies impact all industries including architecture, agriculture, education, healthcare, banking, financial services, news, politics, entertainment, manufacturing, sports, tourism, and transportation—to name a few.

In addition, in every industry, all common business functions such as recruiting, marketing, public relations, sales, customer service, finance, operations, training, and IT (Information Technology) are deeply impacted by the digital revolution as well.
Therefore, whatever your profession and whatever your responsibilities, the digital transformation is impacting your learning, your job, your future, and our entire society.

Like any revolution, this one also has winners and losers. This book will help you end up on the winning side. You can read it to leverage the digital knowledge in your learning, job, and career.

We will talk about the skills you may need to develop in the near future to ride the wave of a digital tsunami.
In addition to showcasing cool applications of technologies in various industries and jobs, We will guide you through sometimes confusing terms and technological definitions. You will learn about:

- Artificial Intelligence
- Internet of Things

- Big Data
- Machine Learning
- Predictive Analytics
- Cloud and Mobile Computing
- Digital Marketing
- Augmented and Virtual Reality
- Drones
- Robotics & 3D Printing
- And much more...

We look forward to guiding you through this unprecedented period in human history when digital technologies profoundly impact the level and quality of our lives while changing and morphing at an astonishing rate in front of our eyes. The main objective of this book is to inspire you about the possibilities of the digital transformation.

You will discover a lot of exciting and innovative applications of the latest technologies in all walks of life. This, in turn, will help you find out what technologies may excite you and how to plan making them a part of your future work or study.

2
Digital Disruption Defined

I came, I saw, I digitized

In this chapter we will define digital disruption or how the digital revolution forces impacted existing companies and their traditional business models.

I came, I saw, I digitized - there is some truth to this paraphrase of Julius Caesar's famous quote, "I came, I saw, I conquered." Yes, some of the new digital companies conquered whole industries in a very short time

'Digital Victors'

- Digital photography   >   Kodak
- Netflix   >   Blockbuster
- Amazon   >   Retail
- Uber   >   Taxis
- Airbnb   >   Hotels
- Social media   >   Print Media
- YouTube   >   TV
- iTunes   >   Music Business
- Online ads   >   Print Ads
- Hard drive manufacturers >   Dropbox
- Camera producers   >   Cameras in smartphones
- Wikipedia   >   Encyclopedia Britannica

Some companies and entire industries either vanished or were marginalized by this digital tsunami. Kodak completely missed the switch to digital photography and Blockbuster to streaming videos. Retailers keep losing business to Amazon, taxis to Uber, hotels to Airbnb, traditional media to social media, TV to YouTube, music recording studios to iTunes, and last but not least, print and TV advertising to online ads.

Hard drive manufacturers got surprised by DropBox and fancy digital camera producers by cameras built into smartphones. Encyclopedia Britannica stopped printing after 244 years, replaced by Wikipedia and the World Wide Web.

New Business Models

- Netflix   >   Blockbuster
- 1 digital song   >   1 CD with many songs
- Streaming anywhere >   Record player
- 1 digital pic   >   36 paper pictures

The disruption was not just technological, either. Digital technology enables completely new business models. The best example is Netflix vs. Blockbuster. The new model is a monthly subscription of unlimited movies for less than $10 without ever having to leave home. The Blockbuster model called for driving to a store to rent a single movie for $3 and having to drive back to return it or pay penalties if one forgot to drop it off.

In the past, we all had to buy a physical album or CD for over $12 with about 10 songs, even if we liked only 3 or 4. With vinyl albums, we were limited to playing it only on a record player—not all of which were portable. Now we can buy any single song digitally and play it on any Wi-Fi or Bluetooth-enabled device anywhere in the world.

We faced a similar situation with developing rolls of film and getting pictures printed. You took a roll of film to a photo shop and got back 36 prints, which, to your dismay, included 30 pictures of very poor quality. This was due to your own steep learning curve on how to master a traditional 35mm camera. Now, we point and shoot with our smartphones without hesitation, check the picture quality, retake immediately if necessary, and post the pic on social media. We very seldom print anymore.

Think About It

"Uber, the world's largest taxi company, owns no vehicles. Facebook, the world's most popular media owner, creates no content. Alibaba, the most valuable retailer, has no inventory. And Airbnb, the world's largest accommodation provider, owns no real estate. Something interesting is happening." Tom Goodwin, TechTarget

This quote makes a very good point that some of the new business models do not even require ownership of physical assets. In all of these cases, the new value provided by these digital companies is in connecting customers with service providers online.

Nothing New

For a perspective on the digital disruption, it is worth mentioning that it's not such a new phenomenon. Walmart became the largest retailer in the world by leveraging telecommunication and by digitizing their supply chain capabilities.

Sam Walton started with one store in Arkansas in 1969, at a time when Sears and Kmart completely dominated retail in the U.S. In about twenty years, it was Walton's turn to dominate the American retail landscape. Kmart is no longer independent, and its parent company, Sears, is not doing very well either. Walmart invested heavily in digital technologies to optimize warehousing, shipping, and pricing. Sears and Kmart missed that trend and paid a very high price for it.

Today, Walmart has over 11 thousand stores in 28 countries and it is the world's largest company by revenue and the world's largest private employer with 2.2 million employees worldwide.

Walmart is not resting on its laurels. It seems to have found a good answer to competition from Amazon. Right now, you can order online anything that Walmart carries and pick it up at the nearest store with no shipping charges. This is especially appealing when purchasing heavy and large items for which Amazon would have to charge considerable shipping fees. Given the vast and very efficient logistics of Walmart, the marginal cost of shipping additional items to any of their stores is near zero.

Agriculture Precedence

There is a lot of fear that digital transformation will result in a lot of job losses and increased unemployment. I could not agree less. Here is why: In 1900, 40% of the total labor force in the United States was employed in agriculture. One hundred years later this number has shrunk to 2%.

At the same time, the total population of the United States increased from 76 million to 282 million— almost tripled. Yet the price of food has gone down so much that even the poor face obesity problems today. How did that happen? Simply put, there was a tremendous increase in farm worker productivity due to mechanization and automation. One good Harvester combine replaced many expensive horses and many expensive workers, and the savings were passed down to consumers. This is how the wealth of the nation was and is being built; i.e., by increased productivity.

Military Precedence

The U.S. military is probably the largest and the most sophisticated digital organization in the world. Even Visa, Walmart, or Facebook cannot come close.

Constant technological inventions force this large institution to adapt to changes all the time. The stakes are very high—it's the freedom of the country in the context of nefarious activities of rogue dictators around the world who do not have democratic processes to stop them from military mischief.

Let's imagine what kind of pressure the invention of an airplane, or a tank, or a missile, or the radio put on our military. They have to keep adapting very fast to develop new weapons, train soldiers, and deploy and reorganize command and control protocols in light of new weapons and communication capabilities.

They have done a great job at that, as the U.S. military put a stop to two world wars in a row in the last century. And today, no other military even comes close to matching U.S. overall global deployment and communication capabilities. If an organization as large as the U.S. military can do it, so should most business as well.

However, most businesses think that they do not face a mortal threat. Unless they are about to be disrupted by the digital transformation. Just ask Kodak, Blockbuster, or Encyclopedia Britannica.

Automation Fears Over the Years

Following are several telling quotes regarding the fear of automation over the last 200 years:

"The rapid industrialization of the English economy cost many craft workers their jobs. Many such unemployed workers, weavers and others, turned their animosity towards the machines that had taken their jobs and began destroying factories and machinery. These attackers became known as Luddites, supposedly followers of Ned Ludd, a folklore figure. The first attacks of the Luddite movement began in 1811. The Luddites rapidly gained popularity, and the British government took drastic measures, using the militia or army to protect industry. Those rioters who were caught were tried and hanged, or transported for life.
Unrest continued in other sectors, such as with agricultural laborers in the 1830s when large parts of southern Britain were affected by the Captain Swing disturbances. Threshing machines were a particular target, and hayrick burning was a popular activity."
Wikipedia

"We are being afflicted with a new disease of which some readers may not yet have heard the name, but of which they will hear a great deal in the years to come—namely, technological unemployment. This means unemployment due to our discovery of means of economizing the use of labour outrunning the pace at which we can find new uses for labour."

*John Maynard Keynes,
Economic Possibilities for our Grandchildren (1930)*

"The rise in unemployment has raised some new alarms around an old scare word: automation. How much has the rapid spread of technological change contributed to the current high of 5,400,000 out of work? ... While no one has yet sorted out the jobs lost because of the overall drop in business from those lost through automation and other technological changes, many a labor expert tends to put much of the blame on automation. ... Dr. Russell Ackoff, a Case Institute expert on business problems, feels that automation is reaching into so many fields so fast that it has become "the nation's second most important problem." (First: peace.) The number of jobs lost to more efficient machines is only part of the problem. What worries many job experts more is that automation may prevent the economy from creating enough new jobs. ... Throughout industry, the trend has been to bigger production with a smaller work force. ... Many of the losses in factory jobs have been countered by an increase in the service industries or in office jobs. But automation is beginning to move in and eliminate office jobs too. ... In the past, new industries hired far more people than those they put out of business. But this is not true of many of today's new industries. ... Today's new industries have comparatively few jobs for the unskilled or semiskilled, just the class of workers whose jobs are being eliminated by automation."

Excerpts from TIME magazine article on February 24, 1961, "The Automation Jobless."

"I am therefore transmitting to the Congress a new Manpower and Training Development program to train or retrain several hundred thousand workers particularly in those areas where we have seen chronic unemployment as a result of technological factors and new occupational skills over a four-year period, in order to replace those skills made obsolete by automation and industrial change with the new skills which the new processes demand."

John F. Kennedy in a speech to a joint session of Congress on May 25, 1961

"Technology is creating both new opportunities and new obligations for us—opportunity for greater productivity and progress—obligation to be sure that no workingman, no family must pay an unjust price for progress.

Automation is not our enemy. Our enemies are ignorance, indifference, and inertia. Automation can be the ally of our prosperity if we will just look ahead, if we will understand what is to come, and if we will set our course wisely after proper planning for the future.

That is the purpose of this commission. I hope and I expect that its work will benefit the workingman and benefit the businessman, and serve the interests of the farmer and the professionals and all of our people in America."

Lyndon B. Johnson, remarks upon signing bill creating the National Commission on Technology, Automation, and Economic Progress. August 19, 1964

In 1978, the historian Ian Turner predicted, that the world was about to enter a period as significant as the Neolithic or Industrial revolutions. He predicted that, by 1988, at least a quarter of the Australian workforce would be made redundant by technological change...

"In the 1980s, new technologies can decimate the labour force in the goods-producing sectors of the economy..."
Barry Jones Sleepers, Wake! a bestseller first published in 1982

However, none of the fears documented above have materialized and in the meantime the whole world got richer, healthier, better educated, and enjoying freedoms like never before.

Since 1820 till today

- The percentage of people living in extreme poverty decreased from over 90% to 10%
- Illiteracy has shrunk from 90% to 17%
- Child mortality declined from 45% to 4%
- The percentage of people living in democracies increased from 1% to 55%

https://ourworldindata.org/a-history-of-global-living-conditions-in-5-charts/

All these impressive numbers were made possible ONLY due to the progress in technologies, that is, automation. It is also worth adding that in the meantime cars, airplanes, telephones, movies, radio, TV, cameras, electricity for homes, air conditioning, refrigerators, computers, the Internet, antibiotics, vaccines, social security, and running water in your tap had been invented.

The way automation and new technologies generate wealth is pretty simple:

1. New technology saves time, hence labor, hence cost
2. The price of a given product goes down
3. More people have more money to spend
4. Since people love to spend when they can afford it, they create demand for more products and services—often luxuries or near-luxuries
5. New products and services are introduced
6. New technologies impact these new products and the original ones as well
7. Back to #1, times the number of new products, which gives us a multiplier of wealth creation

We feel poor when we fail to recall our recent industrial history. For most of humanity—even just 100 years ago—life was drab, short, hungry, dangerous, smelly, sweaty, and dependent on a local despot abusing their subjects in many physical and financial ways

As long as individuals are free to benefit from inventions in a free market, humans will find creative ways to adapt to most circumstances, increasing their own wealth and that of society as a whole.

We should welcome these changes, not fear them. Technology plays a major role not only in wealth creation, but also in eliminating a lot of mundane, boring, tedious, and expensive tasks, leaving time for more value-added activities such as thinking, designing, or spending more time doing the things we love.

Dropping off and picking up dry-cleaning, filling out paper forms, retyping numbers between various systems (and then getting yelled at for making mistakes), looking for missing paperwork, translating, answering phones from unhappy customers, constant scheduling and rescheduling of meetings, sending and answering emails and matching them with text or voice messages, printing invoices, posting content on social media, ordering office supplies, basic cooking, balancing checkbooks, cleaning, lifting, moving, lubricating, fixing, making trip reservations, paying bills, reordering basic cleaning supplies, unnecessary driving, unnecessary meetings, and unnecessary flying (with the associated security delays), retrieving and cleansing data by hand, analyzing spreadsheets by hand, being put on hold by your service provider—all of these tasks can be automated and/or eliminated so we can do something more fun and productive.

Today, most businesses large and small spend at least 50% of their time on the mumbo-jumbo described above. Think about the potential for our economy if we started to produce something instead!

3
Major Players

Let's take a look at the major players in the digital transformation. The five titans are among the top ten largest companies in the U.S. in terms of market capitalization. The history of these companies often reflects the history of the digital transformation itself.

Apple is the largest company in the world in terms of market capitalization. It's bigger than Exxon Mobil, Johnson & Johnson, and Walmart!

Google is barely 10 years old and it's bigger than Johnson and Johnson, which has been in business for over 120 years, and Walmart, which has been around for over 40 years.

Annual Revenue and GDP Comparison

To get a perspective on how large the Internet titans are, we can compare their annual revenues to the annual Gross Domestic Product of entire countries!

Thus, Apple's revenue is equal to all domestic production in Ecuador; Amazon is comparable to Kenya, Yahoo to Mongolia, and Microsoft to Croatia. Isn't that something??

Next, we will describe the major players in more depth.

Apple

- iTunes - disruption of music business
- 1 song or $1 versus a $15 CD
- Illegal copying (not by Apple)

Apple's impact on the music industry was huge. iTunes totally disrupted the music recording business. Digitizing music and selling one song at a time for about $1 instead of a whole album for about $15 was a big shock to the incomes of recording studios and artists.

Recording studio executives did not envision the danger of this new model and almost gave away the farm. The problems were exacerbated by illegal copying of digital music as well, and the lack of enforcement of copyright laws. As a result, today, a lot of famous bands need to keep touring to generate revenue as there is not enough income from selling music online. The winner - Apple and consumers; the losers - recording artists.

- 23% market share worldwide for smartphones
- Losing market share to Google's Android
- Different licensing models

Apple's iPhone had an even greater impact on the digital transformation. The iPhone was a precursor to all smartphones. Its revolutionary design was later emulated by Google's Android. It was the first touchscreen phone, combining camera, microphone, speakers, GPS, compass, vibration sensors, and a vast library of apps developed by independent aficionados.

As of May, 2016 iPhone had about 23% of the worldwide market as compared to about 70% for Android (9). iPhone led the smartphone revolution, but was ultimately surpassed by Android based phones.

Apple did not allow for licensing of its operating system, called iOS, and insists on manufacturing hardware themselves. Google went the other way, giving away its operating system, Android, for free, to any hardware manufacturer around the world as long as they installed some Google properties on it by default. This resulted in a variety of manufacturers around the world driving down the cost of production, which is why Android based phones are considerably less expensive compared to iPhones.

From a user perspective, there is not much difference in functionality and some may even argue that Android phones have a superior user interface. As a result, iPhone is now losing market share. This reminds me the situation with Macs vs. PCs. At that time, it was Apple vs. Microsoft.

Microsoft was licensing Windows to anyone willing to pay for it, while Apple insisted on manufacturing hardware themselves. As a result, Apple had a single digit market share compared to Windows machines.

So, Apple started the smartphone revolution, but now faces stiff competition from makers of Android phones around the world.

- Applications by independent developers
- Initially mostly games
- Today, data collection and transmission hubs
- In 2015, Apple sold > $20 billion worth of apps

Another impact was a new business model whereby iPhone hosts applications written by independent developers for a cut of the revenue. Most apps are just simple games. However, more and more applications are taking advantage of all the sensing and communication capabilities of iPhones and provide a lot of value as data collection hubs. A perfect example is the Nike fitness tracking apps collecting the data from sensors and sending it up to the cloud for comparative analysis with other fitness fans.

Apps contribute about 10% of Apple's total revenue. In 2015, Apple sold over $20 billion worth of apps worldwide.

Google Search

Mainly search engine company
Disruption of print and TV advertising
Almost 70% market share in search

Google derives 98% of its over $60 billion annual income from ads tied to Google searches and YouTube videos.

Google positions itself as a widely diversified technology company, but its revenue split does not reflect it. This includes renaming Google to Alphabet and creating independent business units like the one devoted to driverless cars.

Google's contribution to the digital transformation is significant disruption of print and TV advertising. The Google advertising model was brought about by a very inexpensive and powerful network of computers as well as advanced search algorithms. It is worth mentioning that Google was not the first one to invent or practice this business model. It was the best in commercializing it, though, grabbing a lion's share of the market, currently estimated at around 70% in the U.S.

YouTube

- Changing viewing habits
- The second largest search engine

Another huge Google contribution is YouTube. The viewing habits of the younger generation are switching to watching streaming videos on portable devices instead of cable TV. YouTube is perfectly positioned to take advantage of this trend. YouTube is also the second most popular search engine worldwide.

Android

- Free operating system for smartphones and smart appliances
- Almost identical functionalities to Apple's iOS
- Licensed to many equipment manufacturing companies
- Google Play - similar to Apple's App Store
- Android versus iOS apps

Google controls the Android operating system, but it is not a major source of revenue as the company gives it away for free. Both Android and Apple's iOS are almost identical in functionality. The major difference is in the licensing model. Android is licensed to hardware manufacturers who want to use it; Apple insists on manufacturing its own hardware.

Google also replicated Apple's app store idea. Given the market share of Android devices, all apps on smartphones and tablets need to come in two flavors - iOS and Android.

Facebook

- Social Media - Today The King of the Hill
- Instagram And WhatsApp
- Marketing and technical success
- No immune to competition

Today, Facebook is the unquestioned king of social media and totally dominates this space. In addition to the Facebook platform, it owns the widely popular Instagram and WhatsApp platforms.

In 2015, for the first time in the history of humankind, over 1 billion people around the world were logged in to a single system, and it was Facebook. This is not just a huge marketing success but also a great technological achievement. Imagine the complexity of technical issues supporting 1 billion live connections around the world!

Facebook's strategy is to match all possible features that the competition may offer. Thus, Facebook recently added encrypted messaging and live video streaming, as well as features matching filters on Snapchat.

- Strong competitor to traditional media
- Business model based on revenue from advertising
- Extreme precision in targeting
- Privacy and censorship issues
- Facebook at work

Facebook and other social media are major disruptions to traditional media, especially print. The *New York Times* recently signed a deal with Facebook whereby *New York Times* content is fed directly to the Facebook news feed. This reminds me of when Apple began distributing music. The traditional press had better watch out letting social media distribute their content!

Today, the Facebook business model is mainly based on paid advertising. The value of Facebook to advertisers is substantial as they can target their ads extremely precisely based on detailed user profiles and their activities. So, for example, it is possible to take out an ad that will only be geared toward mothers who are under 40 years old, have more than 2 kids, living less than 20 miles from Legoland, and enjoy Lego blocks. Such precision in advertising combined with its low cost was unheard of only 10 years ago.

On the other hand, Facebook is facing data privacy issues as it tries to balance how much detail it collects against how much it makes available to advertisers.

Facebook is trying to make inroads into corporate America with Facebook at Work. The idea is to leverage Facebook's familiar features such as news feeds, groups, messaging, and events in professional settings, separate from personal accounts.

Amazon

Amazon is the unquestioned king of e-commerce. First, it disrupted the book publishing business to a similar extent as iTunes disrupted music recording studios.

Based on that success, it expanded to selling anything online, including streaming movies where it competes directly with Netflix.

It's worth noting that only about 9% of retail purchases in terms of dollars in the U.S. are made online. Yes, almost everyone has bought something online, but people tend to buy things that are inexpensive and do not weigh a lot as they try to avoid large shipping charges.

It remains to be seen if online retail sales in terms of dollars ever exceed 20% of total volume. People still like to shop in person, especially for more expensive or personal items such as upscale clothing, footwear, furniture, jewelry, and appliances, to name a few.

- King of ecommerce
- From soup to nuts
- From soap to streaming movies
- Data center - cloud services
- Ecommerce less than 10% of total value of retail sales

Wanting to leverage its technical prowess, it started to offer Amazon Web Services (AWS) or cloud computing services. They include storage, networking, analytics, security, and application services, to name a few. Basically, you can run your whole IT department on Amazon hardware and software located somewhere in its numerous, humongous data centers. And you do not have to buy or configure your hardware and software, or face large upfront costs—just sign up, and pay month-to-month fees for the service and avoid capital equipment costs.

In October of 2015, AWS introduced AWS IoT, or Internet of Things, framework. We will discuss IoT in more detail, but the idea is very similar to AWS; that is, Amazon will take care of connecting all the sensors, establishing communication, moving and storing data, and, finally, analyzing and communicating it for you.

- Data centers - cloud services
- Corporate IT services
- Internet of Things

Microsoft

Microsoft almost missed the whole Internet revolution while enjoying the monopoly of its Windows operating system and nice cash flow from Office products. Even Bill Gates did not see the potential of the Internet. However, today, with new management, it has morphed into a competitive, Internet-ready business.

Its Azure cloud platform competes directly with Amazon, including Internet of Things (IoT) and advanced analytics services. It is now handling 300 billion authentications per month.

- Almost missed Internet revolution
- Very strong in corporate world
- Competes with Amazon on corporate IT services

Given that Microsoft products such as Windows and Office can be found in almost every large business around the world, it has a great base to market its digital services. In 2016, it acquired LinkedIn, giving it a nice social media presence.

Microsoft's software 'stable' includes cloud versions of Word, PowerPoint, and Excel; CRM (Customer Relationship Management) and ERP (Enterprise Resource Planning) systems, as well as the popular database SQL Server plus the data analytics and visualization tools. This is more than you need to run 90% of businesses around the world.

And now it also offers LinkedIn, which is used heavily by most job seekers and HR departments.

With the right pricing, I can see a very compelling scenario where IT managers would rely exclusively on Microsoft to furnish all their infrastructure, applications, data, and security products and services.

Given Microsoft's existing relationship with most businesses around the world, the trend toward cloud solutions, and the exploding Internet of Things market (more on IoT later), I can see a nice future for this relatively old technology company.
Leveraging Office and other popular software products
LinkedIn acquisition
Compelling case to take over IT departments

Management Consultants Jumping On the Digital Bandwagon

In addition to the major technology players we just discussed, there are also major consulting companies who are an integral part of the digital transformation and disruption.

It is a sign of the times that, even as big and as powerful as these digital giants are, they cannot do it all themselves. They need to partner with service companies who will implement these technologies.

In the last 4 years, all major technology consulting companies formed separate divisions devoted to digital services. What is new is that the most prestigious management consulting firms such as McKinsey, Bain, and Boston Consulting also joined this trend.

This means that digital transformation issues have finally reached the board and CEO levels. In fact, Digital Transformation tracks were the bestselling breakout sessions at the very influential 2016 World Economic Forum at Davos.

• Digital McKinsey offers a wide range of digital services
http://www.mckinsey.com/business-functions/digital-mckinsey/how-we-help-clients

• Bain Digital promotes comprehensive digital consulting

http://www.baindigital.com/products/

• Boston Consulting Group Digital Ventures has opened 8 offices globally

https://www.bcgdv.com/

• Accenture launches Accenture Digital – 23,000 professionals unit

https://newsroom.accenture.com/subjects/digital/accenture-launches-integrated-digital-capability-to-help-clients-accelerate-growth-through-digital-transformation.htm

• IBM Digital Experience employs 10,000 experts just in digital marketing

http://fortune.com/2016/01/29/ibm-resource-ammirati/

• PwC – 3,000 plus digital business experts

http://www.wsj.com/articles/pwc-pushes-further-into-design-digital-business-1444192201

• KPMG established a Digital & Mobile practice
https://advisory.kpmg.us/managementconsulting/capabilities/technology/digital-mobile.html

• Deloitte Digital – has around 5,000 employees

http://www.deloittedigital.com/

Technology consulting companies invested heavily in this market, as illustrated by Accenture's forming a 23,000-person unit to offer digital services worldwide.

IBM, PwC, KPMG, and Deloitte are not far behind.

Why would so many top consulting companies enter the market of digital services? Here is McKinsey Global Institute's estimation of the market potential.

"In our research for the McKinsey Global Institute, we looked at more than 150 specific digital applications that exist today or could be in widespread use within 10 years and estimate that they could have a total economic impact of $3.9 trillion to $11.1 trillion per year in 2025."

The estimate above does not even include substantial billion dollar revenues related to online and smartphone games and apps, as well as the systems integration needed for cross-functional analysis. To put things in perspective, the annual GDP of the United States is about $14 trillion.

4
Digital Customer
Twinkle, Twinkle Little 5 Stars

In addition to the Internet titans, the clear winners in the digital transformation are customers. There has been a monumental shift in power to consumers and away from producers and retailers.

One can say that, collectively, consumers are major players in the digital transformation. Most digital applications yet to be built will center around making customers' lives even easier.

Customers are already used to rating products and services online using a 5-star scale, and this trend will only grow.

Power Shift

Let's talk about the history of this monumental power shift.

In the past, you had to set aside time for shopping and physically go to a store. With limited hours in a day, you could do only so much research. Your options for price comparison were limited. In most states, for example, car dealers lobbied for legislation to stay closed on Sundays, so you had even less time for comparison shopping.

Yes, there were catalog-based mail order firms like Sears, but the selection was rather limited by today's standards.
There was the *Consumer Report* monthly paper magazine, but it cost money and did not cover many items that may have been less popular.

There was no public forum to log complaints. There was the Better Business Bureau, but who would bother to go there or call before shopping for a pair of sneakers?

- Physical trip
- Restricted time
- Hard to compare prices
- Paper catalogs
- Monthly paper magazines with product evaluations
- No public mechanism for complaints

Connected Customer

Enter the Internet and instant free access to all possible products and their prices. Next, consumers started sharing comments and opinions on products and services on social media.

This put tremendous pressure on B2C (Business to Consumer) businesses. All pricing and product specs, as well as negative and positive opinions, were out in the open.

Next, we witnessed the proliferation of smartphones. Customers carrying smartphones were much more likely to tweet an angry opinion right on the spot as opposed to going home and having to do it on desktops after they had a chance to cool off. The feedback loop became instantaneous.

Amazon was the first to popularize the 5-star rating system for books purchased on their site. This was followed by Apple with 5-star ratings for iPhone apps. Both companies killed the proverbial two birds with one stone. They provided a valuable feedback mechanism to customers and simultaneously a tool to evaluate their suppliers.

Next came Google and Yelp using the by then familiar 5-star system for local businesses such as restaurants, roofers, dentists, physicians, etc.

- Effortless Search and Feedback
- Effortless price comparison
- Effortless product/service public online evaluations
- Smartphones proliferation - instant feedback loop
- Amazon > books
- iPhone > apps

- Google, Yelp

Beware Of 3 Stars

As a result, consumers got used to rating almost anything. This put businesses that had a lot of reviews with an average below 3 stars in real jeopardy.

Consumers simply got spoiled with their power and with the ease of feedback. Therefore, today's customer service needs to be as easy to reach as possible and extremely responsive. In the age of Twitter, few customers will wait 24 hours for an answer. Easy-to-use interfaces on mobile phones, real-time chats, and Twitter support are becoming minimum requirements.

- 3 stars or less spells big trouble
- Twitter effect
- 24 hours response time not acceptable

Customer Experience

The extreme ease of placing repetitive orders as well as providing data on historical purchases is a must as well. Amazon's Dash Button is a perfect example of simplicity in reordering—you can get your detergent with one push of a Wi-Fi enabled physical button stuck with adhesive to your washing machine. You don't even have to go find your smartphone!

This enhanced customer service is now referred to as the 'customer experience', as it includes all of the above plus esthetics and simplicity in the service interaction. Everything being equal, a business with an ugly and hard to navigate customer support interface will lose to a competitor who put a lot of thought into making the interaction as easy and appealing as possible. Customer experience blends digital and physical worlds, and it is a very exciting and growing phenomenon where we see a lot of activity and creativity.

Imagine waiting for service at a car dealership in a crowded, poorly ventilated, and poorly lit room with drab, worn out furniture, a loud TV, stale coffee, and no Wi-Fi. Contrast this with surroundings in your favorite high-end restaurant... The idea is to have a positive impact on all your senses; sight, hearing, touch, taste, and smell.

- Repetitive, similar orders

- History of purchases
- Amazon's Dash Button
- Customer service vs. Customer Experience
- Physical aspect
- Positively engaging all senses

A good customer experience is the ease of returning a rental car where an agent checks you out with a handheld digital device without having to visit and wait at the counter. Managing customer expectations also falls into this category.

A great example here is a progress bar providing the status of your Domino's pizza when you order it online. You know when they put your pizza in the oven and took it out, and when the driver left the store. Another great example is FedEx's tracking number emailed to you when your order leaves the dock so you know when to expect delivery. You can track the status of Christmas gift arrivals just before December 25th.

J.D. Power has long been known for rating the quality of cars. Now they provide 5 level ratings by surveying customer satisfaction with the quality of electronics, financial services, healthcare, insurance, retail, travel, and even sports. With sports, they measure fans' satisfaction with ticketing, arriving at the gate, security, ushers, seating, food, beverage, souvenirs, and how easy it was to leave a game.

Most people like to travel, but few enjoy our airports. If there is a perfect example of a poor customer experience it is security screening. Long lines, no benches to sit down to remove footwear, walking barefoot on cold and dirty floors, no benches on the other side to put your shoes back on, and indifferent stares from agents whose salaries are funded by our tickets but who forgot how to smile. Actually, this negative experience keeps a lot of potential customers from flying, especially on shorter distances when the alternative is driving a car. So, negative customer experience cost airlines… customers. I know that airlines are not responsible for security screening, but their revenues suffer because of poor customer experience at the airports they serve.

- Returning a rented car
- Status bar - FedEx, Domino's Pizza
- Going to a football game
- Airport security screening
- Poor customer experience is very expensive

Spoil Them Rotten

Customer experience is a slightly misleading term. A superior experience is a major selling point to prospective clients who are not customers yet. This includes the promise of fantastic holidays, superior cruises, exciting scuba diving, great golfing, etc.

Thus, for example, Sandals Resorts promises a great experience to prospective customers as a part of their promotions. They promise great experience to get you to become a customer.

Here is a copy of their offer directly from www.sandals.com

Luxury Included® Vacation
FOR TWO PEOPLE IN LOVE
Come experience the very pinnacle of luxury Caribbean all-inclusive vacations with Sandals Resorts. Sandals delights couples in love with supreme vacation packages at <u>luxury resorts</u> in <u>St. Lucia</u>, <u>Jamaica</u>, <u>Antigua</u>, the <u>Bahamas</u>, <u>Grenada</u> and <u>Barbados</u>, featuring gourmet candlelit dining for two, gorgeous <u>tropical settings</u> and some of the world's most exquisite beaches, where <u>golf</u> and <u>scuba</u> are included at each all-inclusive resort.

Keeping Honest

On balance, the shift of power to consumers is very good for both society and the economy. Businesses were forced to be more transparent, less arrogant (think car salesmen), more responsive, and more price sensitive. The fly-by-night operators got weeded out. The best stayed in business and are profitable by providing quality products and services. This is one of the best examples of transparency brought about by digital technologies.

The only businesses that escaped this scrutiny are those who enjoy a monopoly and have little incentive to improve. Nevertheless, the overall increase in business service standards puts a lot of pressure on non-competitive services as well.

- Power shift good for society and economy
- More transparency
- Less arrogance
- Competitive pricing

Royal Treatment

The term 'Customer Experience' blends a lot of familiar concepts, such as:

- convenience (easy to find, park, try & test the product, return, contact, etc.)
- good quality
- personalization
- exclusivity
- ambiance (store or location condition, impression, lighting, character, atmosphere, and even climate control)
- pleasant, professional, and competent personnel
- fast service
- fair price/value
- seamless checkout/payment
- functional, minimal, and esthetic packaging
- efficient delivery
- overall satisfaction

Please note that this does NOT mean low prices. Actually, the better the customer experience, the less need to keep prices low and the better the chances for profitability.

Also, it is worth noting that all the above mentioned attributes span brick-and-mortar as well as online shopping experiences. Thus, customer experience is a blend of digital and physical experiences.

As we discussed before, customers today interact with businesses simultaneously on many channels; in person, via website, smartphone app, phone, text, email, or even traditional mail.

Customers purchase products that may be physical in nature, such as clothing or food, or purely digital, such as movies and songs. Or they buy hybrid products such as smartphones, game consoles, laptops, smart TVs, etc.

Extending and sustaining superior customer experience also blends digital and physical worlds. A great example is a well-designed smartphone app to check into and order room service in a very nice hotel. The same app will also open the room door, let you book a spa, and bill you seamlessly and automatically.

Extending and supporting such experience requires a well thought out digital and business strategy. Actually, it is getting harder and harder to distinguish one from the other. Technology drives new possibilities in the traditional physical world, as illustrated with the hotel example. Poor or spotty wi-fi coverage is not acceptable in a luxury hotel. On the other hand, the best wi-fi connectivity will not assure a customer's satisfaction when faced with dirty bedding, rude room service, and substandard food.

As the population grows more affluent, it expects more pampering from all retailers. This in turn raises the bar of expectations with respect to level of service in business-to-business or consumer-to-government transactions. Thus, the need to provide the best possible customer experience forces everyone to increase the level of service regardless of the type of industry or the size of the business.

The winners are customers, but this trend to keep spoiling them cannot be supported in traditional ways. Hence, the pressure by all businesses to leverage digital technologies to keep up with the competition. This is one of the major drivers of the digital transformation in businesses; i.e., having to constantly invent and/or catch up with new ways to attract and retain customers who are only going to be more and more demanding.

The good news for businesses is that a lot of these customer service related ideas, technologies, and processes are very similar, regardless of the type of business, size, and industry. Thus, all businesses can be inspired by studying other industries which, in the past, would not make sense to compare with. Case in point: chatbot support by smartphone can be used by any business of any size in any industry. The same goes for a good quality website integrated with a customer database that is itself integrated with smart email marketing and a social media management system. So, a small local coffee shop stands to learn how to treat customers from a global manufacturing conglomerate and vice versa.

Frequently, when we think about customers, a retail experience comes to mind; i.e., I've entered a store so I am a customer. However, customers are also:

- Students, for schools
- Students, for individual teachers
- Teachers, for school administrators
- School administrators, for vendors and service providers

- Patients, for doctors
- Doctors, for hospitals
- Hospitals, for insurance companies
- Insurance companies, for software vendors
- Pet owners (and pets themselves) for veterinarians (better make sure that Fido doesn't suffer during a checkup :-)
- Applicants for government services (permits, taxes, fees)
- Voters, for politicians
- Voters, for community organizers
- Congregations, for clergy
- Local tribes, for missionaries
- Golf players, for caddies
- Sport celebrities, for advertisers
- Members, for trade associations
- Readers, for authors and publishers
- Parents, for children
- Children, for parents
- Spouses, to each other

Thus, in our lives, we are both customers and suppliers. Simultaneously, we wear the many hats of customers and suppliers every day.

A teacher commuting to school in the morning is a customer of the school district (not just an employee), publishers (teachers decide on book adoptions), the local transportation system (they use the roads that better be well maintained), and a local coffee shop (assuming they enjoy a morning shot of caffeine). At the same time, teachers are suppliers to students, parents, school districts, the community, and their own family.

These multiple roles expose us to various customer experiences and raise the overall bar of excellence. It is perplexing and thought provoking to consider why we would be treated like kings or queens by one establishment and as a pariah by another in a span of just a few hours. We all want to be treated royally all the time. And this is one of the major drivers of digital transformation; i.e., increasing affluence and the expectations that come with it.

5
BENEFITS OF DIGITAL TRANSFORMATION
A Triple Play

Let's talk now about three major benefits of the digital transformation.

They are related to:

1. Measuring phenomena that existed before but have never been measured, as the cost of measuring was prohibitive
2. Measuring more frequently and precisely, thus automating and optimizing processes that existed before
3. New products and services that did not exist before

Benefit Type 1: Market Research and GPS

Twenty years ago, there was no way to count how many times people searched for the best barbeque grill before they decided to purchase one. Today, Google records every instance of every phrase typed into the Google search box by anyone in the world, with a detailed breakdown by city, date, and demographics. This may not be important to you personally, but it's very important to the producer of BBQ grills trying to estimate the demand for their products over 12 months in Florida versus Minnesota.

Another example is GPS recording our geographical coordinates every second. Hence, we know where we are, we know the optimal way to go, and we can estimate how long it will take to get to the destination. 30 years ago, everyone carried a lot of maps in their glove compartments. A lot of turns and exits were missed while driving. How many paper maps have you seen lately?

GPS brings tremendous value to businesses that operate fleets of cars or trucks. It is now possible to account for every car or truck all over the country and to be able to optimize their routes— thus shortening delivery cycles, saving on fuel, and better managing driver fatigue.

The third example in this category is wildlife tracking with GPS collars to better understand the behavior of the species and thus to better manage our natural resources. Or to track our puppy Fido who wandered away.

Benefit Type 2: Automation and Optimization

Manufacturing processes have existed for many years, but they were not always measured, controlled, and automated to the extent possible today.

A great example here is the fully controlled, mostly automated, and highly optimized production assembly of modern cars. Today, Smart produces about 100 cars per employee per year. In the 1930s, Ford built 10 cars per employee per year. Keep in mind that Smart is much more complex when compared to 1930s-era Fords.

Another example is the almost fully automated production of beer including bottling, packaging, and warehousing.

It's worth noting that the benefit of measuring can materialize only when the cost of measuring is less than the benefit of measuring itself. This quote perfectly depicts this quandary: "Not everything that counts can be counted, and not everything that can be counted counts." We do not know for sure who said that, but it's frequently attributed to William Bruce Cameron or Albert Einstein.

Love and friendship are impossible to measure. There is also no point in measuring the number of grains of sand in a sandbox, even if we could do that. The digital transformation provides great tools, but they do not substitute for or digitize thinking, sound judgment, and common sense.

Benefit Type 3: New Products and Services

The third benefit of the digital transformation is the creation of completely new products and services that did not exist before. This includes the digitization of pictures and sound, which enabled 3D modeling, 3D printing, computer games, virtual design and testing, and virtual and augmented reality. This category also includes new combinations of software, hardware, and telecommunications. For example, smartphones will interface with robots, smart cars, drones, advanced analytics, etc. This category represents the most exciting and the most promising benefit of the digital transformation.

Additional Benefit: Increased Transparency

It's our strong belief that digital technologies are catalysts for increased transparency, and thus to greater accountability in business, politics, education, news, nonprofits, sports, entertainment, health care, politics, and government. This is one of the greatest benefits of the digital transformation. We will discuss why we think this trend is here to stay.

There are two camps as far as transparency is concerned. The first one believes that transparency is the currency of the Internet and practices it daily, building their brands based on trust. The second camp may pay lip service to accountability; however, it may have no choice but to slowly embrace it. Thus, it's my belief, that, on average, digital technologies are a significant contributor to the gradual increase in building more trust and subsequently leading to a more productive and civil society.

Trust, in addition to its moral dimension, also has a very beneficial practical aspect; that is, it lowers the cost of doing business. It's obvious that the more people trust each other, the more productive and the longer their collaborations will thrive. Simply stated, a mutually trusting relationship leverages each person's strengths, wasting little energy watching their backs. The whole is just greater than the sum of its parts.

Benefits Summary

The overall benefit of the digital transformation is an increase in the level and quality of human life. The affluence and freedom of societies is directly tied to our overall productivity. On average, if we want to be twice as rich, we need to improve our productivity by a factor of two. One of the best ways to achieve this is to digitize, measure, automate, and optimize.

When we're not producing, we need to recoup our energy with engaging activities and entertainment. The digital transformation is making sure that our leisure time is filled with a plethora of options including games, easy-to-access reading, movies and music, less-stressful driving, and a great, relaxing customer experience when we fly, visit national and theme parks and museums, eat at restaurants, and stay in our favorite resorts.

PART II
INDUSTRY IMPACT INDUSTRY IMPACT

1
INTRODUCTION

In the following chapters, we will review the impact of the digital revolution on many industries. We will concentrate on each industry's specifics and discuss the current status as well as potential.

For many reasons, industries vary a lot with respect to digital maturity, but none can ignore the underlying digital trends. Usually, these reasons are not technical; the differences are more related to financial and organizational constraints.

For example, the media industry output is today almost all digital - news, TV, online magazines. Thus, one would expect them to be heavily digitized. On the other hand, agriculture or construction, and especially smaller operations may not be able to afford digital tools, as they do not have economies of scale comparable to large media companies.

As discussed before, one common major challenge, regardless of industry or size of the business, is to provide a superior customer experience.

Also, all industries share several common processes such as recruiting, marketing, public relations, sales, finance, and IT.

Thus, it makes sense to discover how each industry copes with these trends. And then learn about various digital strategies and apply what is most relevant to your business.

2
DIGITAL RETAIL
WWW = What I Want, When I Want, Where I Want It

The retail industry has been heavily impacted by the digital disruption and it is still trying to figure out the optimal balance between brick and mortar stores versus online shopping.

Some companies like Nordstrom and Victoria's Secret have successfully navigated the stormy retail waters. Many went out of business or lost independence: Kmart, Circuit City, CompUSA, RadioShack, Borders, County Seat, Fashion Bug, Kids "R" US, Osco Drug, Phar-Mor, Frank's Nursery & Crafts, Builders Square, B. Dalton, Hollywood Video, and F.A.O. Schwarz, to name a few of the best known.

In general, regardless of the channel, retail consumers are seeking a great experience and are expecting that they will get what they want, where they want it, and when they want it.

The first digital challenge to traditional retailers was the emergence of e-commerce sites. The trend picked up the pace in the mid-1990s with the advent of better security, online credit card processing, faster connectivity, and better graphical interfaces, which all came together to provide a reliable user experience. It was the time when Amazon, eBay, and PayPal were doing serious trailblazing in the field of e-commerce.

- E-commerce is born around 1990
- Amazon, eBay, PayPal
- Credit card payments online
- Better connectivity

Now, about 20 years later, over 60% of Internet users in the U.S. buy products online. However, online retail sales account for less than 9% in terms of total dollar value of retail sales.

Conclusion: a lot of people shop online and they may be buying a lot of products, but they do not spend a lot of money. This means that they tend to buy smaller, less expensive goods. This is not surprising, as the cost of shipping is still a major roadblock to online purchasing.

Online shopping is great for low-risk products such as books, cosmetics, or household cleaning supplies, linens, pet food, and dry foods such as tea or coffee. On the other hand, it is unlikely that you would buy a high-end wedding dress, diamond ring, or fancy leather jacket on Amazon.

60% of people shop online but...

- Online sales less than 9% of total retail sales by value
- Online sales of smaller, less expensive items
- Books, cosmetics, cleaning supplies, dry food
- No diamond rings or wedding dresses

People still like shopping in person, especially for high-end goods with the potential for sentimental value. Shopping also has social value, as it allows people to interact with each other on a regular basis, such as during a weekly grocery trip.

The jury is still out whether online shopping will ever exceed 30% of the total retail value of sales for the combination of reasons described above. Nevertheless, it is a sizeable portion of overall retail sales and it is exposed to digital transformation forces.

People like to shop in person

- Luxury
- Sentimental value items
- Large gifts
- Social interaction

One of the biggest challenges is how to incorporate multiple digital touch points with prospective clients to understand how they make buying decisions and what is the best strategy for promotion.

Let's discuss this very typical scenario: I see a product promotion briefly on my smartphone. The screen is too small to look at all the details. Upon returning home, I grab a tablet to show the product to my spouse. My spouse loves it, but has a specific question about the product detail that can only be displayed well on my large desktop screen. I go to my desktop and after a careful examination of colors, size, and detail, I decide to preorder it and pick it up at the local store. I do it on a desktop as I prefer filling out all the pre-order information using a keyboard over one-finger pecking on my tablet.

I go to the store and before I pick the preordered item up, I get an e-coupon for a competitive product beamed right to my smartphone. This happened because I opted in to be tracked in the store and my smartphone has a record of my searching and looking for the original product.

The offer beamed to my smartphone is so good that I cannot refuse it. I walk up to a shelf but... then I notice a third, unadvertised alternative, which, upon close inspection, beats the previous two. I decide to buy the third alternative right then and there and I pay cash.

Multiple digital touchpoints

- Smartphone
- Tablet
- Desktop
- Visit in a store
- Drawn by Product A but deciding on Product X

This is a very challenging scenario for all involved. In the retail industry, it is called the attribution challenge. Who gets the credit for this sale? Manufactures of the two first products paid for the promotion and tracked me very closely. But the third manufacturer got a sale with almost no effort; however, that third manufacturer and the store itself have no idea about my demographics because I paid cash.

This multi-device, multi-location phenomenon makes it hard to analyze retail consumer behaviors and thus the effectiveness of promotions.

- Attribution challenge
- Who gets the credit?
- Hard to analyze customer behavior
- Hard to analyze promotions

WWW is not a World Wide Web anymore...

In general, consumers are seeking a great customer experience and are expecting that they will get what they want, where they want it, and when they want it.

To that effect, Home Depot has invested over $1.5 billion to make the mobile buying experience as easy as possible. Home Depot built their ordering system to communicate with the IFTTT framework. Therefore, you can set up a text or email alert to be sent when the price changes at Home Depot or when the back ordered item is on its way to a store or home.

- Great customer experience expected
- Consumer expects to get
  - What they want
  - Where they want
  - When they want

In general, there are several different specifics with respect to brick and mortar versus online retail. The online model allows for more control and analysis of promotions and less overhead, but it is very competitive. The brick and mortar model involves much more capital and provides less control regarding promotions, but it has the advantage with more expensive, larger, and upscale goods.

A lot of brands are pursuing hybrid models whereby shoppers can order online and pick up in the physical store or have it delivered to their home. Or they can order items in the store that are back ordered and have it delivered later.

- Brick and mortar vs. online specifics
  - More capital, less control over promotions
  - More expensive items
- Online specifics
  - Less capital, more control over promotions

o Less expensive items
- Hybrid models

E-commerce or not to E-commerce

In addition, many manufacturers of consumer products face the e-commerce question: "Should we sell our products directly to consumers over our own e-commerce website?"

Case for e-commerce

- Increased revenues
- Higher margins
- Direct contact with consumers
- Keeping up with the digital Joneses

Case against e-commerce

- Cost of implementation and maintenance of a new e-commerce site
- Shortage of e-commerce/Internet marketing skills
- Possible conflict with existing distributors
- Stiff competition from Amazon and, soon, Alibaba
- Competition for ranking in search engines for generic products

There are several risks that come with e-commerce. Some disadvantages include: the cost of implementation and maintenance of a new e-commerce site, shortage of e-commerce or Internet marketing skills, and a possible conflict of interest with existing distributors who may not appreciate competition from their own supplier.

For most generic products, there is very strong competition from Amazon, which has humongous sales volumes and thus corresponding purchasing and negotiating power. There is also great competition for generic products to show up on the first page of Google.

Getting e-commerce right is complex and expensive.

- Evaluate pros and cons
- E-commerce works well for unique brands

- But probably not for larger things...
- ...you want to touch before you buy
- One Kings Lane

Before jumping into e-commerce, you may want to evaluate the above pros and cons. Given stiff competition from established e-commerce powerhouses, it is very hard to succeed with generic products. However, there is a great opportunity for niche products and services such as luxury branded clothing or art. Nordstrom and Victoria's Secret are doing very well online.

On the other hand, let's take a look at One Kings Lane, an e-commerce company that sells home décor and furniture but does not manufacture it. It has raised over $200 million in capital since its inception in 2009. As of 2016, though, One Kings Lane was still unprofitable. Valued at $1 billion several years ago, it is now worth only about $150 million.

- Consumers are in almost total control
- WWW customer or bust

In the summary of retail digital challenges, one thing is certain. Customers equipped with smartphones are in control and they will give business to merchants who do the best job getting them what they want, where they want it, and when they want it. And digital technologies are perfectly equipped to grant this wish. We know a lot about what customers want. And we should be able to deliver it to home, office, store, or anywhere else at the desired moment.

Thus, if a customer says 'I want this dog food to be delivered to my doorstep this weekend, or I want my AC filter to be ready for pickup tomorrow morning, or I want this lunch buffet to be set up in this conference room a week from today at 11:25, we can meet these expectations with no effort and a big smile while enjoying healthy profits.

Digital Retail Technologies

Retailers can run their businesses smoothly with the assistance of technology like radio frequency identification devices (RFID) tags, QR codes, location-based beacon technology, smart price tags, smart shelves, smart shopping carts, digital signage, and data analytics tools.
With a smart price tag, retailers can change the price of items from their computer. They do not have to create another tag and re-tag all of the items

on the shelves. This will lead to more competitive and efficient inventory control.

With beacons, retailers can also monitor the time spent by each customer at the most visited areas. Using sensors and beacons in their outlets will further improve store layout and merchandise placement strategies, leading to new business strategies.

Smart carts tallying total purchase value combined with mobile payment systems can reduce wait times at checkout and reduce security requirements for handling cash without unloading and loading carts at checkout.

Last but not least, manufacturers and retailers can help reduce their costs associated with a recall or product contamination, as they would be able to easily and quickly locate the impacted products, suppliers, and customers.

- RFID tags in every garment
- QR codes
- Beacons
- Smart tags
- Smart shelves
- Smart shopping carts
- Digital signs

Costco customer experience

Have you shopped at Costco lately? I like that store's merchandise and prices, but what I do not like is that they change the location of items and there is no store map to find particular merchandise. And on weekends, there are long lines at checkout and a person at the exit checking my receipt (another line).

Today I have no alternative, but if I found a similar store that offers me a smartphone app guiding me to the right aisles to find things I buy every week (supported by nice screens on the shelves to confirm I am in the right place) and if my shopping cart could know what's inside and accept my mobile payment, I would switch immediately.

Almost every time I shop at Costco I get irritated by the fact that I cannot find my repetitively purchased products and I have to stand in two lines to get out of the store.

How sustainable is that customer experience?

- Constant change to location of items
- No store map
- No clear signage 0n shelves and what's on them
- No mobile payments
- Checkout lines
- Checking receipt on exit line

3
DIGITAL HEALTHCARE
Physician, Digitize Thyself

Healthcare is one of the least digitized industries (McKinsey graph here) in the U.S. At the same time, healthcare costs are spiraling up due to an aging population, the lack of market mechanisms, and the exorbitant cost of new drug development.

- Aging population
- Lack of market mechanism
- High cost of drug development

Nevertheless, there is great potential for improvements on 3 fronts; optimization of existing business processes, remote diagnostics, and new medical treatments enabled by digital technologies. Let's discuss them one by one.

Better processes

There is no technical reason for paper records in medicine anymore. Unfortunately, this is the reality today. The major disadvantage of paper processes is related to the manual recording of information. This leads to many errors due to false readouts of cursive, misplacement, damage, the lack of an automatic audit trail, and the lack of remote access, to name a few.

Paper is not a good media for such important and life-dependent documentation. Existing cloud systems with constant backups, redundancies, and privacy protection are better alternatives. Until recently,

they may have been too expensive. Today the cost of making mistakes based on handwriting may be higher.
Procedure and patient scheduling is another time consuming aspect of medicine. Endless hours on telephone hold are wasted trying to line up the right resources in the right place at the right time.

There is no technical reason for paper prescriptions anymore, either. Better data collection and analysis would improve clinical decision making and reduce the need for redundant exams.

"A recent study revealed that medical errors are the third-most-common cause of death in the U.S. after cancer and heart disease, accounting for more than 250,000 deaths every year."
Martin A. Makary and Michael Daniel, "Medical error—the third leading cause of death in the US," *British Medical Journal*, May 3, 2016.

How many of these deaths were related to poor quality of records or records not being available in the right place at the right time? We may never know, but it's reasonable to expect that a significant percentage of these unfortunate cases could have been avoided with better and more timely digital records.

- No technical reason for paper records
- Manual processes are error prone
- Paper records are not searchable
- Medical errors - the third-most-common cause of death
  - Illegible
  - Missing
  - Not accessible on time

Remote diagnostics and care

Remote patient monitoring and diagnostics has great potential to provide improved access and quality of healthcare at significantly lower cost.

"Nearly half of all adults in the U.S. (117 million people) suffer from chronic conditions with nearly 58 million suffering from 2 or more. 86% of the total cost of total U.S. healthcare is related to these chronic diseases. Heart conditions, chronic obstructive pulmonary disease, asthma, and diabetes constitute the largest cost component.
These conditions also have the greatest potential for using digital remote medical monitoring to improve patient outcomes, and reduce costs."

Gerteis J, Izrael D, Deitz D, LeRoy L, Ricciardi R, Miller T, Basu J. Multiple Chronic Conditions Chartbook.[PDF - 10.62 MB] AHRQ Publications No, Q14-0038. Rockville, MD: Agency for Healthcare Research and Quality; 2014.

The federal government is already reimbursing patients for this virtual, "non-face-to-face" monitoring for Medicare patients for 19 chronic conditions.

Internet connected blood pressure cuffs, EKG sensors, electronic weight scales, glucometers, spirometers, and other devices are the basis for virtual care real-time. They provide actionable patient information directly to healthcare providers. Such information is the basis for individual patient alerts specific to their condition and medications.

Providers set up nursing teams to respond immediately to changes in patient vital signs. This helps to avoid expensive and medically unnecessary readmissions while improving patient care.

Essentia hospital in Minnesota has reduced hospital readmissions for congestive heart failure from the national average of 25 % to less than 2% simply by connecting an electronic weight scale remotely to the hospital's alert system. Weighing patients every day helps greatly to identify real problems. But coming daily to the hospital just to be weighted is inconvenient and expensive, so patients skipped these basic diagnostics.

http://www.healthcareitnews.com/news/essentia-health-slashes-readmissions-population-health-initiative-telehealth

According to a Goldman Sachs report, joining the physical and digital worlds and changing physician and patient interaction through digital healthcare "offers the most commercially viable potential to change the U.S. healthcare economy."

Goldman Sachs estimates over $305 billion in savings due to 3 new innovations:

$200 Billion from remote patient monitoring
$100 Billion from telehealth - remote diagnostics, counseling
"An infinitely large savings" from lifestyle changes to address obesity, smoking and exercise.

Roman, DH and Conlee, KD, (2015), The Digital Revolution Comes to U.S. Healthcare, Technology, incentives align to shake up the status quo. Goldman Sachs Global Investment Research, Internet of Things, Vol. 5. (June 29, 2015.)

A home lab

Here is a powerful example of simple and inexpensive digital medical devices already on the market, all connected with each other and your smartphone while storing and analyzing your health data in the cloud.

The Philips Health Watch can be used by patients with chronic conditions, such as hypertension. The watch shows users steps, calories burned, active time, and sleep time. This $250 watch also comes with an optical heart rate monitor and accelerometer, which tracks varying heart conditions through an accompanying smartphone app.

It knows when you were sitting too long and instructs you to stand up and move!

- 4 sensors
- Weight
- BMI
- Fat percentage

A $99 body weight device measures, monitors, and motivates users to change habits. It is built on the same Philips HealthSuite digital platform, an open, cloud-based platform that collects and analyzes data.

- Blood pressure
- Heart rate

The $99 device measures blood pressure and heart rate. It's also integrated with the cloud based health monitoring application.

- Fast measurement in 2 seconds
- One press of the button

This thermometer is $59 and is also synced with the rest of the devices.

- Free from Accu-Check
- Integrated with smartphone and cloud

•

This wireless and connected glucose meter is available free from Accu-Check.

In summary, for less than $500 you could have a powerful mobile home lab for cardio, blood pressure, weight, temperature, and glucose recording, all conveniently stored, displayed and analyzed for you. This is the equivalent of 2-3 doctor visits. However, using it and analyzing results may save you a lot of money, pain, or even your life.

In medicine, like in all other industries, Pareto's law applies; i.e., 80% of problems are caused by 20% of possible reasons. These 4 devices can help you manage 80% of your health problems for $500.

- Cardio
- Blood pressure
- Weight/BMI
- Temperature
- Glucose levels

And if you are diabetic, these 5 devices may be all you may need to monitor your health without frequent doctor visits.

Looks like a super bargain to me!

New treatments enabled by digitization

The third category of benefits of digitization is related to new treatments and products enabled by progress in digital technologies. We will discuss 3D printing, robotics, ingestible sensors, nanosensors, and finally, DNA sequencing.
We will review the most interesting developments in each area.

3D printing in medicine

3D printing fits well with medicine. Most applications are precise, custom one-off creations, and the speed and cost of printing is not a critical issue.

he most popular applications include custom hearing aids. When you visit a doctor, they take the 3D parameters of your ear opening and pass them to a device manufacturer for a 3D printing job. As a result, you get a perfectly fit hearing aid.

Another usage of 3D printing is in preparation for complex surgeries. For example, it is being used in the separation of Siamese Twins. The medical technicians render a detailed plastic 3D printed model of the parts to be separated. Surgeons can then plan and practice the best way to separate tissue, bones, and, blood vessels.

The next category of 3D printing application is in reconstructive surgeries. Imagine repairing damage to a skull; the relevant parts can be 3D-printed and implanted.

Watch this fascinating video on 4 applications of 3D printing in medicine. They range from being able to practice for a complex surgery to bone reconstruction, and custom implant creation all the way up to printing actual organs.

Complex surgery preparation, practice on 3D model, production of custom fit hearing aids, bone reconstruction, implant printing, Biodegradable implants:
https://www.youtube.com/watch?v=y87RmyBxKic

Organ 3D Printing:
https://www.youtube.com/watch?v=G0EJmBoLq-g

Robots

Robots are the fusion of very powerful computers, sensors, and precision mechanics. They have a lot of potential in healthcare.

There are two major applications of robots in medicine. The first are robotic prosthetics. They enable the replacement of lost limbs and making them communicate with the patient's brain, thus restoring the basic functions of arms and legs.

The last category involves the actual organ printing. It is now possible, for example to print a new ear for you (in case you lost it or just want to improve your appearance).

Nothing can describe the state of the art of robotics and the potential better than this video:
https://www.youtube.com/watch?v=KPhkVPNKtVA

Another robotic application is used to supplement a skilled surgeon. A surgeon sits in front of a magnifying screen showing the patient while operating the machine's robotic arms with video game-like controls.

The robot arms can get into hard-to-reach places, cause less bleeding, decrease the chance of damage to important nerves, and reduce the size of incisions and scars compared to traditional surgeries. All of this adds up to much shorter recovery times.

The higher cost of operation is offset by much shorter recovery time, which can run thousands of dollars per day.

With reliable connectivity, it is conceivable to perform surgery anywhere in the world as long as the surgeon's console can communicate in real time with a robot. In the future, all procedures can be taped and all the parameters of the procedure can be stored in the database. This data combined with the data on surgical outcomes, may help in training and improvements in repeatable standard processes.

- Surgeon 'playing' a video game
- Robot gets to hard-to-reach places
- Less chance of damaging nerves
- Less bleeding
- Smaller scars
- Faster recovery

Ingestible sensors

Proteus Digital Health provides a diagnostic system based on a smartphone, a patch and a pill. Pills contain a one-square-millimeter sensor that is coated in two digestible metals. After swallowing, the sensor is activated by electrolytes within the digestive system. The signal from the pill is transmitted to a battery-powered patch worn on the user's torso. The patch sends the data via Bluetooth to a smartphone. Such systems can be used to analyze the chemical composition or our digestive system in order to uncover abnormalities.

- One square millimeter sensor
- When swallowed, sensor is activated by electrolytes
- The pill transmits a signal to a small patch
- Patch communicates with smartphone

Another example of ingestible sensors is the camera pill—a miniature camera that can be swallowed to take and transmit images of internal organs.
The PillCam is used as an alternative to standard colonoscopies. The miniature camera can detect polyps to identify the first signs of colorectal cancer. The battery-operated pill takes high-speed photos and sends the

image to a device outside the body, which then forwards it to a computer for diagnostic analysis

Nanosensors

The future may belong to nano-sensors, or miniature sensors so small that they can travel in your bloodstream and communicate test results to your smartphone. They can detect cells that are shed from the inner lining of arteries—precursors of a heart attack that are hard to detect with any other tests.
This is a perfect example of what is possible at the confluence of major digital revolution drivers, miniaturization of sensors, ease of data transmission, and data analysis.

DNA sequencing

DNA is the essence of life. It carries genetic instructions played out from the moment of conception until death, and determines our height, intelligence, eye color, hair, what disease we may die from, etc. These instructions are coded in a DNA chain comprising billions of combinations.

Knowing our DNA helps us learn where we came from, how organisms are related, and how they evolved. In practical terms, the knowledge of DNA is instrumental in finding cures for diseases, preventing epidemics, and last but not least, identifying somebody based on traces of their remains or to determine paternity.

If a Google search is looking for a needle in a haystack, then DNA sequencing is akin to comparing all the straws in the haystack to every other straw, and putting them in order of similarity. Since a 'DNA hay stack' has billions of combinations, it requires very powerful computers to do all this sorting, comparing, and matching.

Progress on DNA research is directly tied to the computing power of computers. This is a great example of the contribution of the digital revolution to the understanding of life and extending it (at least in the physical context).

In very practical terms, the knowledge of your own DNA can help in early detection of a possibly fatal but curable or preventable disease. Thus we should be grateful to computer scientists as much as we are to medical researchers and doctors.

Summary of Digital Healthcare

- Better Existing Processes - especially medical records
- Telemedicine
- 3D Printing
- Robotics
- Mini sensors
- DNA sequencing

4
DIGITAL TRANSPORTATION
On the digital road again...

There are two types of transportation: personal and commercial. Let's discuss both.

Personal transportation

On the personal front, our cars are full of software and connectivity. Dashboards on new cars today are pure software; they have Wi-Fi connectivity and hotspots, and can stream videos to multiple screens built into the passenger seats. We are connected to GPS, satellite radios, and IFTTT applications (If then this then that). Our smartphones are integrated with speakers and internal microphones. We can locate and unlock our car from anywhere.

- Wi-Fi hotspots
- GPS
- Satellite radio
- IFTTT interfaces
- Bluetooth smartphone integration

Most cars manufactured today have a standard interface for engine diagnostics and their mechanical components are integrated with the software. It's come to the point that hackers can now break into your Jeep and stop it dead in its tracks. A routine part of Tesla maintenance is a software update.

- Car diagnostics on board
- Crash avoidance
- Detecting fatigue
- Self driving cars

Radar and laser technologies are involved in crash avoidance warnings. Unusual blinking of driver's eyes can detect driver's fatigue.

The next step is a self-driving car

The case for self-driving cars is very compelling on many fronts. I do not expect them to eliminate driving by humans. I see them complementing it.

For example, on a long trip I may give up control on a long stretch of a highway but I want to have the fun of driving on a nice winding country road. Or go off road in my Jeep. Too many enthusiasts are unwilling to give up the joy of driving. But the same enthusiast may use a self-driving taxi when traveling in an unfamiliar town or neighborhood, or having free hands to finish the PowerPoint presentation at the last minute.

Self-driving cars can ease the stress of long daily commutes and provide more time for work or entertainment.

I can see self-driving cars doing the last mile delivery to homes for services such as food or package delivery to save on labor cost.

They are ideal for people with disabilities who cannot drive themselves, but do not want to be driven for financial or privacy reasons.

- Complementing human driving
- Long stretches on highway
- Easing daily commute stress
- Last mile deliveries
- Disabled, elderly, sick

Self-driving trucks and tractors in agriculture can address the shortage of skilled drivers during the peak season.

In addition, one third of over-the-road transportation cost today is labor. This creates a very strong incentive to minimize it as much as possible.

When the technology is tested and mature, self-driving cars will have the potential to decrease collisions. Human error is a factor in almost all accidents.

Today the closest thing to a self -driving vehicle is the automatic pilot on passenger jets. Highly qualified pilots cede control of big airplanes with hundreds of passengers, so they can rest during long stretches of intercontinental flights.

Last but not least is the potential for self-driving cars to address traffic and parking problems in large cities. With mature technology, I can envision congestion optimization algorithms guiding self-driving vehicles to reach destinations in optimal time. We may be 20 years away from that scenario becoming a reality, but wouldn't it be nice if we could at least ease our traffic jam frustrations and save time and money in the process?

- Addressing labor shortage
- Driving the cost of transportation down
- Increasing safety
- Decreasing congestion and traffic problems

Confluence with insurance

As discussed in the Financial Services module, there is a very interesting confluence of digital applications between transportation and insurance industries. By taking advantage of the same tracking capabilities, Progressive Insurance launched a usage-based-insurance program offering up to 30% discounts depending on how frequently and how well you drive. Progressive customers agree to have the tracking devices installed in exchange for lower premiums. The additional benefit to Progressive is the collection of traffic data to assess the risk of particular locations during a specific time of day or weather based on the data from many customer vehicles.

- Discount to you depending on how well you drive
- Data analytics for insurer to better assess risk

Commercial transportation

On the commercial side, there is even more integration and communication. Fleet management systems also do predictive analysis on part failures and alert the service affiliates about the upcoming service while transmitting information on the required parts.

RFID chips attached to loads get scanned and invoices are generated automatically upon delivery after the pallets with goods are offloaded.

- Fleet management in real time
- Predictive maintenance
- Route optimization
- Integration with billing

Disrupting taxi monopoly

On the taxi front, Uber discovered that there is $400 mln market instead of $200 mln in San Francisco. Enjoying their monopoly, taxi services ignored half of the possible market. Uber did nothing more than connect riders with drivers.

The Uber model faces some regulatory pushback in many municipalities and countries, but I hope it will survive. In the meantime, it's one of the best examples of digital technology dislodging a complacent monopolist just with information. This would not have been possible before the advent of smartphones as the Uber model depends on easy and instant access to your private phone.

- Uber "discovers" $200 mln in San Francisco
- Breaks up monopoly
- Unthinkable before smartphones

Smart containers

You may ask what sushi, strawberries, and pharmaceuticals have in common. They all travel around the world but need to stay in refrigerated containers to make a long trip. These three types of cargo will not tolerate even a few hours of heat.

- Sushi/Sashimi
- Fresh raspberries
- Pharmaceuticals

Smart containers at sea

Maersk, one the largest shippers in the world, has a fleet of over 250,000 refrigerated containers, known as reefers. Today, about 60% of the claims made against Maersk relate to failures of reefer units. This number will go down with the new tracking. Another benefit is the ability to certify the quality of products and support it with audit trail data.

- Refrigerated containers - reefers
- Real time tracking and logging
- Location
- Inside temperature
- Inside humidity
- Off service
- Can certify quality

Smart containers on the road

There are an estimated 15 million trucks in the U.S. Approximately 2 million of these are semi tractors with about 5.6 million accompanying trailers. Many of these are refrigerated trucks that assure the fish, raspberries, and pharmaceuticals can make it to the final destination in refrigerated condition.

- 15 million trucks in the U.S.
- Real time tracking
- Some of them carry the smart refrigerated containers
- Extension of overseas shipping
- Assuring end-to-end temperature control

Food safety

The Food Safety Modernization Act is the most sweeping reform of U.S. food safety laws in more than 70 years. It aims to assure the safety of food throughout the supply chain through the introduction of new requirements for food manufacturers, processors, transporters and distributors. The idea is to ensure the U.S. food supply is safe by shifting the focus from contamination response to prevention.

Most shippers have until March of 2017 to comply with these new regulations. Companies with less than 500 employees have at least 1 additional year.

The new act requires that the shipper must be able to provide a log of the controlled environment upon request from the receiver or an auditor. These records must be kept for a period not exceeding 1 year.

With perishable foods requiring refrigeration, it is almost impossible to comply with this law without real time temperature monitoring. In this case, government regulations almost force digital control, real time monitoring, and a digital audit trail.

- Food Safety Modernization Act of 2011
- Involves
  - good manufacturers
  - processors
  - transporters
  - distributors
- Preventing contamination
- Audit trail - logs to be kept for 12 months
- Almost impossible to comply without real time monitoring

Cargo vessels - no crew

"All hands on deck" may no longer apply.

Advances in automation and satellite bandwidth make it possible to design and build cargo vessels sailing the oceans with minimal or even no crew. British engine maker Rolls-Royce is working on a crewless ship. The designers are tapping know-how from those working on driverless cars.

A future ship would be equipped with infrared detectors, high-resolution cameras, and laser sensors to monitor its surroundings. Vast amounts of data would be transmitted via satellite to command centers. It is estimated that unmanned shipping could cut transport costs 22%.

Until recently, lack of affordable bandwidth has made it impossible. A new generation of communications satellites transfers data at much lower cost than in the past.

- Rolls Royce future no-crew cargo ship
- Optimize ship use
- Cut labor cost
- Possible due to advancement in automation and satellite communication

Disrupting FedEx?

Nobody is safe from the digital disruption. The last company I would expect to be digitally disrupted is FedEx.

While on the surface, Amazon is still a great partner for FedEx, Amazon could turn its own vast shipping infrastructure into a business—like it did with its cloud network, turning it into Amazon Web Services, a computing platform that is popular with large American companies that decided to use Amazon's expertise in managing large computing operations. Amazon AWS customers include Netflix, Airbnb, Expedia, Adobe, Pinterest, Yelp, NASA, and Comcast among others.

Amazon is facing increasing pressure to lower delivery costs and increase the immediacy of deliveries for its Prime service members. So, Amazon is introducing its own 40 branded cargo planes. It already has transport trailers, and a program called Flex that uses everyday drivers with their own vehicles for last-mile deliveries.

Long term, Amazon is working on a drone-based delivery fleet, and it's also looking into driverless cars in a possible partnership with Fiat Chrysler. Amazon may not need FedEx anymore. Instead, look for them to compete with FedEx and the USPS.

- Watch out FedEx
- Amazon leases own planes
- Has own ground service, Flex
- Drone delivery in the future?
- Vast logistical infrastructure including data analysis

Amazon restaurant delivery

Amazon has recently introduced free one-hour restaurant delivery to Prime members in Houston, TX.

Restaurants include Carrabba's, El Tiempo Cantina, Max's Wine Dive, Thai Gourmet, The Hay Merchant and many more.
Using Amazon's smartphone app or from desktop computer, you can browse menus, place orders, track the delivery status, and watch as the delivery courier travels from the restaurant to the delivery address in real time.

After all, Domino's Pizza has built a billion dollar business on food delivery, so the market is already there.

- Amazon Prime members in Houston can use free one-hour restaurant delivery
- Restaurants, include Carrabba's, El Tiempo Cantina, Max's Wine Dive, Thai Gourmet, The Hay Merchant and many more
- On an app, you can browse menus, place orders, track the status of your delivery, and watch as their delivery courier travels from the restaurant to the delivery address in real time

Transportation Summary

Transportation and logistics offer a lot of examples of the benefits of digitization. A lot has already been done, as a lot of our personal and commercial vehicles are already connected and thus traceable and even serviceable from any place with smartphone coverage.

All the collected data is already being used to optimize routes, assure quality of perishable goods, reduce delivery times, and minimize transportation costs.

Self-driving vehicles are the next frontier that can further drive the cost of transportation down and make commuting safer, more relaxing, and less congested.

Issues regarding the management of congestion in larger cities are discussed in more depth in the Digital Government section.

- Every vehicle, truck, ship, plane can be connected
- Remote diagnostics
- Route optimization
- Supply chain optimization - from producer to consumer
- Quality audits
- Regulatory compliance
- Cheaper, faster delivery
- Safer, fresher food
- Self driving vehicles
- Managing congestions and safety

5
DIGITAL TOURISM
'The fool wanders, a wise man travels'
Thomas Fuller

In tourism, everything is about customer experience. You go on vacation to relax, reduce, stress, make as few decisions as you can, and enjoy your precious time off.

Disney has probably done the most to accomplish that goal by leveraging digital technologies throughout its operation. Disney's MagicBand is the epitome of the stress-less customer experience. You get a wristband that opens doors, orders food in advance and pays for it as well as for souvenirs, guides you through a theme park, and, most importantly, helps to avoid long lines for your favorite rides and attractions.

You can program your MagicBand 30 days in advance with your attractions and ride preferences. An accompanying smartphone app will guide you and minimize the wait time among hundreds of rides and attractions. MagicBand is tied to your credit card so you do not have to carry a wallet with you. There are no tickets, passes, check-ins, or other hassles. You get your wristband in the mail a week in advance and your magical experience starts at the airport where Disney picks you up in a van and handles your luggage for you. From then on, the MagicBand does all the magic described above.

Inside each wristband is an RFID chip, radio (like on a cordless phone), and a battery. The sensors are spread around the whole park and this is how your presence and your preferences are detected.

Behind the scenes is powerful software and hardware coordinating communication between sensors to understand where you are, what you are doing, and what is coming up next. It cost $1billion and took 3.5 years to implement. The project started in 2008. Today, it may be less expensive to develop, as many technologies involved in the project got cheaper.

- Disney leveraging digital technologies
- MagicBand
- Complex digital system
- $1 billion and 3.5 years to implement

Customer Experience Turbocharged

This Disney model is an intellectual model for the customer experience. Remove all the friction points, minimize the number of steps and decision points, notify in advance, and require nothing more than showing up.

Any large museum, national or theme park, resort, or golf or country club could use a similar approach. They needn't have all the bells and whistles of Disney's MagicBand, but they can provide simple services such as ordering in advance. They do not have to cost billions, as they can be based on smartphones and beacon technologies that were not available to Disney 8 years ago.

For example, some country clubs offer smartphone based apps that alert service workers about the proximity of presence and display a patron's name and picture on service workers' phones. Thus a server can greet a guest using their last name and check on their preferences for types of refreshments. The app is based on smartphone communication with beacons spread throughout the club's rooms. The app 'knows' at any given time which room a member is in.

- End-to-end hassle-free should be the motto in tourism.

If you buy a first class ticket, Virgin Airlines will pick you up in a limo and usher you through a VIP security checkpoint, check your luggage, and drive you up to the gate so you don't have to schlep through the airport. After you enjoy all the expected amenities of a first class flight, they provide that same assistance upon your arrival, including dropping you off at your selected hotel or destination.

I understand that this is a very expensive option, but any business should think about Disney's and Virgin Airlines' programs as models of customer experience; that is, hassle-free convenience with a smile.

- Intellectual model
- Remove all friction & hassle, minimize decision making
- Similar technology is cheaper today due to better smartphones and beacons
- Country club experience
- End-to-end hassle free
- Virgin Atlantic experience

Tourism is very dependent on good digital marketing practices described in the Marketing section of this book. In a nutshell, any tourism related business has to have a great presence on mobile, be very easy to share on social media, use a lot of videos, and carefully manage its reputation online.

People go on vacation to relax and brag about it later, so the tourism industry needs to make sure that these two basic needs are met.

- Digital Marketing best practices apply
- Great presence on the Internet
- Ease of sharing on social media
- Videos
- Reputation management

Summary

During travel to new destinations, tourists are glued to their smartphones and what they find on smartphones is basic knowledge about almost everything that surrounds them. Hence, any tourist business needs to be easily found and highly presentable with an extremely easy-to-use mobile phone user experience. Especially during vacation, users are not going to spend a lot of time on searches of convoluted, poorly designed websites.

Bookings, reservations, ticketing, and redeeming points or awards should all be easily available and executable on smartphones.

Check-in, check-out, room selection, viewing property layouts, ordering room service, making restaurant reservations, renting equipment—all need to be available via smartphones as well.

Resorts, cruises, conferences, or any venues where people stay longer and may not mind downloading an app, may consider developing their own smartphone applications to make sure that the basic information is available, even if there is no Internet connectivity. Such apps may feature tie-ins with local partners such as limo services, Uber, restaurants, etc.

In 2015, Hilton spent over $500 million to provide such functionality across 650,000 rooms in more than 4,000 properties worldwide.

- Almost total dependence on smartphones
- Easy to find
- Easy to use
- Bookings, reservations, ticketing, check-in, renting, ordering
- Smartphone apps with tie-ins to local partners
- Hilton $500 million investment in mobile experience

6
DIGITAL EDUCATION

'Intelligence plus character that is the goal of true education'
Martin Luther King Jr.

In education, digital technologies have two distinct impacts. The first one is for the instructional technologies used in class by a teacher. The second one is when technologies substitute for a teacher. Sometimes they overlap.

Instructional technologies

Let's discuss instructional technologies first. Interactive collaboration online with a teacher and fellow students is one example. Another is any mechanism that collects feedback, such as clickers, Twitter, and online surveys.

Students can prepare presentations using desktop tools such PowerPoint or Keynote and present them on smart boards. Internet-connected smart boards can display all types of content from text to voice and video. Robotic, augmented reality (aka AR), and drones can be a part of instruction as well.

- Collaborative online
    - o Discussion groups
    - o Emails
    - o Surveys
- Clickers
- Twitter
- Smart boards

- Robotics
- Virtual reality
- Drones

Google offers free Google mail and document accounts for teachers and students to organize and maintain instructional materials. There are also numerous educational apps available in Google and Apple stores. Some of them are geared to specific disabilities. Digital instruction's appeal to students is its ability to be customized for various learning styles. The possibilities here are endless and constantly evolving.

- Library of apps for various learning styles
- Google, Apple apps

Online instruction - student perspective

The second category is when digital technologies substitute for teachers altogether. This is a kind of online instruction that is growing by leaps and bounds. Let's discuss the pros and cons of online instruction, as well as the drivers of this unquestionable trend.

The advantages of online instruction are various. One of the major benefits is that online courses cost much less than instructor-led classes. The cost of course development may be spread among many students, and multiple instructors can teach one class.

The second major advantage is the convenience of worldwide 24/7 access. For students who work jobs to pay for college, this is a major advantage as they do not have to worry about scheduling conflicts.

Students can also study at their own pace and refer to the materials anytime and any number of times as they need. This is not an option with live instruction.

Online content can leverage the knowledge and experience of the best instructors. No more inexperienced TAs teaching 300 students at a time in a crowded auditorium. The best professor can address all the students all the time.

Online instruction can be very rich in a variety of formats and include seamless switches between text, audio, video, and interactive tools such as pop quizzes enforcing understanding of the material.

Online courses provide a level playing field. No one knows your accent, looks, gender, race, nationality, religion or political affiliations. No chances for classroom domination by smart aleck classmates.

Written and traceable communication between students and instructors requires strong written skills and forces more thought and intellectual discipline than off-the-cuff verbal exchanges.

All reference materials including online videos are easily indexed, searchable, and accessible at any moment. This is not always the case with paper handouts.

- Less expensive than live instruction
- No instructor charges
- No room charges
- Convenience - no travel - accessible 24/7 worldwide
- Individual pace - repeatable
- Leveraging the best available instructional talent
- Interactive, various formats - text, video, audio
- Level playing field - no discrimination, no monopolization of discussions by most vocal students
- Written traceable participation requires more intellectual discipline
- Easy access to online reference materials

Online instruction - administrative perspective

From the administrative perspective, the major advantage is the central management of all curricula including usage statistics.

Imagine having historical information on all courses offered including students' time on task, level of participation (number of dropouts, number of interactions) and final results in the form of percent correct answers or problems solved. This would be a great way to evaluate and modify online courses based on meaningful measures.

Last but not least, the commonly shared benefit is the lower cost of instruction to the school and students. This is not a trivial benefit in these times when student debt is growing to worrisome levels.

- Central administration of all curriculum

- Central effectiveness analytics
  - o time on task
  - o participation
  - o % correct
  - o student evaluations
- Lower cost

The major disadvantages of online instruction relate to the lack of personal interaction among instructors and classmates. Online instruction also de-emphasizes the need for verbal communication, which is a very important skill. Some online platforms minimize this disadvantage by providing conference call service to support discussion of group projects.

- No relationship with instructor and classmates
- De-emphasizes verbal communication

Future of online instruction

Online instruction is especially relevant for several groups of students. It's perfect for continuing education of motivated professionals who want to learn at their own pace. It's also great to explain the basic concepts of almost any subject to middle school or older students. There is no question that a good video instruction of, for example, history of any country (including pictures, live interviews with experts, historical footage), would be superior to a blackboard lecture by a single classroom teacher.

However, a discussion of historical context, motives of historical figures, or prevalent value system would be best left to an experienced history teacher.

Thus we think that the future of online education will be a hybrid one. Where it makes sense, and where the presence of a teacher does not add much value, online instruction is perfect. A great example is how to learn Excel. If it's a good program, you do not need a teacher and you can pick it up at your own pace. Online instruction can also involve collaboration and online testing.

But when you need to learn how to prepare a balance sheet and income statement from raw data and how to interpret the information in your spreadsheet, you may greatly benefit from the experience of a live accounting teacher. We also believe that such teacher instruction could be taped and the whole course archived for future reference by all students who graduated from that school.

There is one more hybrid model, where a teacher is on a location *and* accessible via video conferencing technologies to large remote audiences watching the instruction live. This is a great way to leverage the talent of top teachers who cannot be everywhere. It can be preceded by the online prerequisite intro with basic terminology, for example.

In summary, digital instruction tools will evolve at par with office productivity tools, and the future of online instruction is a hybrid of live and online delivery depending on the need for practical hands-on participation.

- Continuing education
- Basic concepts - instructions
- Hybrid 1 - asynchronous online + class discussion + asynchronous online archives
  - Intro online in preparation for class discussion
  - Class discussion videotaped
  - All class materials available online until graduation or even later

- Hybrid 2 - synchronous online with instructor + asynchronous ongoing online forum
  - Live instruction delivered via video conference
  - Live Q & A
  - Live ongoing follow up forum moderated by instructor (LinkedIn or Facebook like closed groups)

Educational Analytics

All education efforts could and should be tracked for a student in a similar way that health records are maintained.

One day, any student as well as their parents and teachers, should be able to access a full history of all courses, instructions, grades, learning styles, skills, aptitudes, participation, psychological assessments, absenteeism, disciplinary problems, etc. (subject to encrypted, well-guarded privacy like health records are subject to). Together with health records, it would give any educator, parent, or student a good idea on what curriculum and circumstances have shaped the student's current level of achievement.

Such data, assuming protection of privacy, could be a goldmine to benchmark what programs work the best. Today, this data is very hard to get and precludes the optimization of teaching and learning.

Nevertheless, even tracking the first two metrics such as time-on-task, and percent correct answers could provide valuable feedback to all involved. The first metric is very hard to compile if instruction is not tied to digital delivery, as it would require time consuming manual input from teachers.

Such analytics would be the major contributor of the value of digitization to the benefit of digital education. It would lead to less expensive and more effective outcomes. Just like in any other industry.

Imagine, too, a global, centralized database of all college credits earned by all students that aggregate as one and requiring no "transfer of credits" from one college to the next. For the many who earn college degrees in non-contiguous sessions and multiple institutions of higher learning as jobs and residences change, this one concept could greatly reduce the cost of tuition and the amount of time to graduate. After all, isn't Accounting 101 essentially the same wherever it's taught?

- Time on task
- Engagement
- % correct
- Progress
- Interventions
- Benchmark
- Portability of records

7
DIGITAL ENTERTAINMENT
Disruptors at the gate

"Disruptors at the Gate" would be a good way to describe how the digital revolution impacted the music and movie businesses.

The music recording business was completely disrupted by Apple iTunes. Lured by the prospects of easy, worldwide distribution, the recording studios made a dangerous deal on two fronts.

First, they decided to distribute one song at a time. This cannibalized the sale of $15 albums. In the past, listeners were just forced to buy the whole album even if they wanted only one song from it.

Second, they became dependent on a distribution channel they did not control.

A third, unrelated fact was that digital piracy has not been curtailed.

The confluence of these three factors led to fewer sales. The winner was Apple, who had no revenue related to music at all prior to this deal. The other winner was customers who saved a lot by not having to buy albums for $12 or more.

Revenues went down so far that a lot of bands, who previously relied on a predictable stream of royalties, found themselves having to tour to make money.

- Total disruption of the business model
  - o One song at a time
  - o Dependence on channels with no control over pricing
- Piracy problems
- Winner > Apple and consumers
- Losers > Studios and artists

Since then, most of the same music is available on Spotify, Pandora, Amazon, and now, YouTube.

Impact of YouTube

YouTube is further pushing down artists' profits. It hired a former MTV director in 2015, signaling a serious commitment to the music business.

From now on, it's not how many records you sell but how many times your music is viewed on YouTube. Very different metrics. Given the importance of YouTube, for many recording artists, YouTube is more important than traditional music studios.

The music business is not the only one exposed to the forces of the digital revolution.

Hollywood started to cast actors not based on their Hollywood credentials but based on the number of followers on YouTube. Is Brad Pitt going to be disrupted by the latest YouTube star who is less expensive but equally appealing?

Hollywood is also experimenting with distributing films as streamed video-on-demand, leveraging the vast social media following.

- Casting YouTube stars
- Leveraging social media in promotions

We discussed how Netflix disrupted Blockbuster. However, Netflix and Amazon are now challenging Hollywood movie studios with their own movie production. *House of Cards* was a great movie-making success for Netflix. Is Hollywood the next to be dislodged by Netflix and Amazon movie studios? Even if it's not going to be dislodged, it is surely being disrupted.

- Bypassing movie theaters
- Netflix and Amazon as movie studios

The importance of social media

Entertainers live and die by social media. Twitter is a must for anyone dreaming to reach the top. Katy Perry has 70 million followers on Twitter. The new and upcoming entertainment stars need to be on social media, especially YouTube.

Sometimes I think that social media were made exclusively for celebrities and their fans.

The former can brag about every bit of trivia every hour and the latter seem to have insatiable appetites for gossip and celebrity self promotions.

- Twitter
- Instagram
- Snapchat
- Facebook

Streaming

Traditional TV watching habits are shifting to watching YouTube streaming clips on any device.

Nevertheless, cable TV still insists on charging $150 per month for 300 channels when Netflix is $8 a month for unlimited movies.

The streaming technologies are pretty mature already.
Microsoft Azure brought the 2016 Olympics to millions of viewers across all devices, including connected TVs, for the first time. Across NBCOlympics.com and the NBC Sports app, there was a record total of 3.3 billion streaming minutes (live + full event replays + highlights).

The major advantage of streaming is that one can watch content on any device at any time (including live feeds). This means the convenience of watching on a tablet in bed, on a smartphone while waiting in a coffee shop, for kids on a built-in monitor on the back of a car seat, or on a big screen TV in your living room with friends.

- Streaming is moving mainstream
- Mature streaming HD technology
- Microsoft facilitated streaming 3.3 billion minutes of Rio Olympics
- Streaming allows viewers to watch on demand, on any device
- Paradox - digital disruption impacts digital products

Summary

The traditional entertainment business has been on the receiving end of the digital revolution. Music and movie businesses became less profitable, streaming took over, and the power shifted toward consumers and new online distributors.

This situation reminds me the shift from traditional print media to social media. The impact on both industries is profound and very painful for those who did not see the trend coming.

Paradoxically, this is in large part due to the digital nature of their final product—everything these two industries provide can be digitized and distributed digitally. It did not help that streaming technologies got so good that one can watch a movie in HD over Wi-Fi. This has changed listening and watching habits and disrupted business models even further.

In retrospect, no one should be surprised with the outcome, but frankly, few saw it coming while it was happening.

8
DIGITAL SPORTS
Golfing in the Cloud

The Professional Golf Association PGA TOUR is the world's foremost golf tour and host to some of the world's top golfers. Its headquarters is located near Jacksonville, Florida.

A combination of wearable and traditional cameras, GPS, military-grade radar, 3D gaming technologies, high-speed networks, and smartphone and tablet apps allows the PGA TOUR to gather an enormous amount of real-time data. The data ranges from live video feeds all the way to the trajectory, speed, and rotation of each shot by every player.

- Wearable cameras
- GPS
- Military-grade radar
- 3D gaming
- High-speed data networks
- Smartphones and tablets

This data is then aggregated and disseminated to TV networks, on-site flat panel displays, analytical applications for players and coaches, and smartphone apps for attendees.

Data collection and analysis

Since every stroke and its parameters are tracked and stored in vast cloud-based databases, each professional golfer can take advantage of their own statistics to improve their game by analyzing each stroke. The amount and granularity of the data collected is staggering. I've never thought about golf in the context of such detailed analytics. This valuable data is also being sold to golf equipment manufacturers to improve their products as well as to enthusiasts of golf who study statistics.

- To improve game - players and coaches
- To sell it to golf equipment manufacturers
- To sell it to golf aficionados

Enhancing customer experience

Mobile apps allow tour spectators to interact socially with each other and the Tour headquarters. Mobile, wearable cameras used by golfers enhance the viewing experience of TV audiences. Analytics play a crucial role in providing historical and comparative statistics on smartphones to avid fans of golf as well as real-time stats on huge flat-panel displays and network feeds for TV viewers. The same data that improves customer experience helps professional golfers improve their game and can be sold to third parties who support the players. And all this data and information is stored somewhere in the cloud. You can say that one can kill four birds with one set of data:

- Athletes and coaches
- Fans on the ground
- TV networks
- Equipment manufacturers

This is a perfect example of the convergence of social media, mobile devices, data analysis, and cloud technologies providing a superior customer experience. In this case, customers are athletes, fans, TV networks, and equipment manufacturers.

- On mobile apps
- On the ground
- On TV

Other sports also take full advantage of real-time multi-camera recordings, instant replays available to coaches, collecting enormous amounts of statistics, and enhancing the customer experience by providing great live close-ups on Wi-Fi enabled tablets for fans sitting in the bleachers.

- Football

- Basketball
- Baseball
- Tennis
- Soccer
- Volleyball
- Many others...

All this detailed footage and statistics make coaches and athletes more productive and accountable, and watching sports more fun. After all, how could you follow a small golf ball on TV without the colorful trace (which trajectory is stored in the database for further analysis)? There is a lot of fun in watching instant HD replays of great shots or plays from many angles in football, basketball, tennis, volleyball, and soccer, to name a few sports disciplines.

With the advancement in streaming technologies, all this footage can be beamed on demand to any connected device. This includes live streaming of events as well. It all increases the viewership of sports events even further, with all the corresponding advertising revenues associated with it.

9
DIGITAL NEWS
All the news that's fit to stream

The media holds tremendous power and is considered a 4th branch of the U.S. Government.

Move over ABC, CNN, NBC, CBS, *New York Times*, *Washington Post,* and other mainstream media. The Internet titans are coming... These are the new players. The King is dead, long live The King!

- Apple News
- Facebook Feed
- Yahoo News
- Twitter Trends
- YouTube Videos
- Google Search
- LinkedIn Pulse

The digital revolution completely disrupted the old media model and the news industry only because the cost of publishing on the web is so much less, that even individuals were able to publish their content and be heard.

Various news strategies

Apple has a nicely designed News app, so there is no longer a need to open several applications to stay informed. Apple has editors on staff who curate the content.

Apple's approach is different than Facebook's, which is providing the news based on algorithms driven by preferences set by users without intervention by experienced editors. For example, if you decide to share your interests with Facebook, you will be presented with matching news content automatically.

Google News and Google Search are integral parts of the new media as well. We go to Google Search frequently to get all the articles on the latest news published on the web.

Facebook, Yahoo, Twitter, and YouTube have made significant progress on the news front already. Given Apple's strengths, it remains to be seen who in Silicon Valley is going to dominate the news business in the future.

- Apple curates the content
- Facebook (supposedly) has algorithm
- Google News and Google Search

Facebook recently struck a deal with *The New York Times*, among others, to embed the news into their feed. The idea is to deter Facebook users from leaving Facebook to get news directly from publishers' websites. *The New York Times* may have decided that they did not have a choice. Given the amount of time people spend on Facebook combined with their unwillingness to leave it to be informed, the iconic publisher caved in.

This reminds me of the risks music publishers took with iTunes. Needless to say, Apple completely disrupted the traditional music recording business. Are traditional news organizations falling into the same trap this time with Facebook?

Several other publishers decided to disable comments on their websites and publish their content on Facebook first. Thus, readers comment on articles on Facebook instead of the *original* website. This has a lot of advantages but also carries tremendous risk. What if Facebook takes issue with both content and users' comments?

Yahoo used to pay Katie Couric $10 million per year to be the face of Yahoo news. This signifies Yahoo's commitment to the news business, a key factor in the company's survival of recent corporate turmoil.

Twitter is already in the news business in a big way with major mainstream media players promoting their Twitter handles everywhere they can, including during live broadcasts of their own shows.

Google's YouTube is in the news business in a big way, especially with the younger crowd that does not watch a lot of mainstream media either on cable or traditional TV. A YouTube channel subscription is already the preferred way to get information among 18 to 24 year-olds.

LinkedIn is promoting its version of news with Pulse, a publishing platform. Like everyone else, LinkedIn tries to 'glue' their subscribers to their content, thus increasing the amount of time users spend on their site. The more time they spend, the more likely they will engage. The more they engage, the more likely ad revenue will increase.

- Facebook & NYT agreement
- iTunes moment for news publishers?
- Comments on Facebook only
- Yahoo - Katie Couric $10M deal
- Twitter as a springboard to all news
- YouTube disrupting traditional TV
- LinkedIn Pulse

The good news for advertisers

It's now possible to measure what content resonates best with users, where they spend the most time, and what kind of news is of interest to whom.

This has been very hard—almost impossible to gauge with traditional print or TV news. Such precise measurements lead to better service and more efficient allocation of advertising budgets.

It's worth noting that advertisers have footed most of the bill for the birth of the digital revolution. All social media and search engine businesses have been based on a model where participation is free for exchange of information leveraged by advertisers to promote goods and services. This is not a different model than existed before when print media and traditional TV were major beneficiary of such revenues.

The total ad spend, or expenditures on advertising in the U.S., was $187 billion in 2015. Digital ads accounted for one third of this figure but it's growing at an annual rate of 13%. The TV advertising spend was 42% of the total or nearly $80 billion; now it's down about 2%.

Comparing these general numbers does not tell the whole story. Clickable digital ads are much more effective per dollar spent as compared to TV or print ads due to the very precise targeting it enables. This is especially true for ads related to search or online behavior. The ads are shown only to people who already expressed some interest in the offer or a subject. On TV, ads are shown to a less qualified audience.

Therefore, the more relevant number to compare would be the total purchases per dollar spent on advertising. It is safe to assume that TV ads are between 5 to 10 times less effective in generating revenue per dollar spent. Given that assumption, the real impact of digital ads on commerce is much larger than when measured by a percentage of total spend between TV and digital.

- Good news for advertisers
- Precise ad targeting (unlike billboards)
- Advertising partially paid for digital revolution
- Impact of digital ads on commerce larger than TV and print combined

Competition

The competition in the news business gives more choices to customers. The younger generation is moving away from traditional news channels.

Never before has the public had so many choices. All parts of the political spectrum have their unrestricted representation on the Internet and they compete with each other at what looks like a completely open market. Traditional media, especially TV, is still quite influential, but it's losing its power as reflected in the grossly diminished revenues from advertising. In summary, the Internet increases public participation and media transparency.

The disturbing trend is that the new media titans are de facto monopolies. censorship.

Facebook and Google are in trouble with EU antitrust regulators who are rightly concerned about the monopolistic position of these organizations.

On the other hand, social media are free to customers, so it's hard to make a case about monopolistic price gouging. The stronger antitrust arguments relate to limiting competition.

- More choices
- More transparency and competition...

- Social media morphing into old media

In summary, social media are morphing into the traditional—but Internet based—media. It's power game, after all. The more things change, the more they remain the same.

10
DIGITAL POLITICS
Democracy 4.0

The digital revolution did not spare the political landscape.

In politics, social media increases transparency. Every post of every candidate can and will be archived by the competition forever (even if it's later deleted).

Imagine our future politicians, today's millennials, 10 to 15 years from now, running for public office. All their social media posts and the entirety of their Internet presence (such as various websites and social media accounts they may have run over time) will be in the public domain for scrutiny by both their opponents and voters at large.

How many current politicians would be holding office today if social media had been around for the last 40 years?

- Social media transparency and scrutiny
- Harder to flip-flop
- Very hard to hide inconvenient facts

Freedom Of Information Act

In addition, we have laws in the U.S. to insure freedom of information both on the federal and state levels. The Freedom of Information Act (FOIA), passed on July 4, 1966, allows any citizen to demand that the records of government operations be disclosed. These laws cover financial and medical records, schedules, meeting minutes, and email usage while conducting official government business.

When the law was passed over 50 years ago, and you invoked this law, you received boxes of paper documents that would be hard to analyze and distribute. Now, thanks to the Internet, after the release of any documents, they can be made public to all in no time for their scrutiny.

So, it's getting harder and harder to be less transparent with all the digital accountability being around. The digital revolution is not going to eliminate all accountability issues overnight, but it will improve it gradually. Politicians, being aware that all their posts on any social media are being archived forever, will need to adjust their communication strategies.

- Freedom Of Information Act
    - o Medical records
    - o Emails
    - o Schedules
    - o Meeting minutes
- Even more pressure on transparency

Directly to voters

On the other hand, social media allow politicians to make better contact with their constituents. Smart politicians know how to use Twitter to take their message directly to voters and supporters. They also use Twitter to clarify their points, and enhance their message. News media are no longer the only conduit between candidates and voters. This must hurt the news folks, but the winner is the public at large.

- Twitter and direct contact with voters
- Media lost a lot of control
- Public is a winner

Digital marketing dependence

Like with media, entertainment, and nonprofit sectors, the digital impact on politics is in marketing and mainly social media. Today's politics require the difficult job of coordinating messages and staying on message across all traditional and social media as well as websites, through email, text, chatbots, and in online ads.

In the recent U.S. Republican primary, a candidate using only Twitter defeated a candidate who ignored Twitter but spent over $100 million on TV ads.

Recently, the president of Turkey, Recep Tayyip Erdogan, effectively saved his presidency as he was able to beam a message calling for support via FaceTime on his iPhone during an attempted coup d'état. iPhone saved his life and his job.

And last but not least, Twitter made a significant contribution to toppling regimes during the Arab Spring.

In democracies, social media are very important in getting voters to the polls. Better social media skills are credited with the Democratic presidential victory in 2008. The Democratic party did a better job energizing their youthful base on social media to go out and vote than Republicans did.

In dictatorships, you'd better watch out for Twitter.   One way or the other, in politics, you ignore social media at your peril.

- Single Twitter account wins with $100 mln budget
- Single FaceTime session saves the presidency
- Twitter speeds up toppling regimes

Digital voting?

Will we ever vote with smartphones? Maybe, but only after we address issues with security, privacy, and audit trails.

Technically, if I can manage my bank deposits and withdrawals on my smartphone, I should be able to vote using my iPhone. Voting via the Internet is easily traceable and can be tallied immediately at virtually no cost.

Facebook has just recently announced that they had 1 billion users logged in at the same time. So, the technology exists to count the choices of 146 million Americans registered to vote.

After all, 99% of registered voters in the U.S. have smartphones already.

The ease and transparency of such a voting process will probably translate to more frequent voting and/or referendums, especially on the local level.

In the past it was hard to get to vote given very large territories and distances— thus the high cost of participation (voting and being informed). These two factors are no longer the issue–we can get all the information we need anytime we need it, and more people could vote more frequently.

- Technically feasible but not organizationally
  - o Privacy
  - o Security
- It would be great but we are not ready yet

The future

Before we vote with smartphones, we may want to consider what was proposed by Pia Mancini in Argentina. You can watch her wise and eloquent TED talk on YouTube.

https://www.youtube.com/watch?v=NXfYNdapq3Q

Her idea is that elected representatives should interact with their constituents on social media forums using a platform they created and called DemocracyOS (similar to closed groups on Facebook or LinkedIn).

The job of a representative would be to translate the legalese of convoluted bills written by lawyers for lawyers to everyday language. And to provide analysis, recommendations, listen to feedback, and engage in online debate among only his constituents.

After that, a representative would submit the bill for an online vote among his constituents only. Representatives would be bound to vote in Parliament according to their own referendum results.

I admit I like this idea a lot. It would force representatives to be more responsive and engaged and the same would happen to constituents. Today, citizens have no easy way to engage with their own representatives, nor do they have a way to debate much among themselves.

This would be a major disruption to the existing model and it is not going to happen overnight. But this is a very noble idea. With the slow generational shift to more voters who are digital natives, I can see this happening in 10 years somewhere in the world... and then spreading globally. Imagine...

- Net Party in Argentina
- Each bill is interpreted and presented for vote
- Referendum online
- More engagement, more accountability

11
DIGITAL GOVERNMENT
To Digitize, To Protect, and To Serve

The role of the government is to protect and serve. It is much easier to deliver on these promises when governments are digitized.

The advanced technologies that only big cities could afford are getting less expensive all the time. Smaller cities can start using them to better serve and protect their citizens.

Car as a platform

The overarching trend is to make a police car a communication platform for officers and to equip officers with a single mobile device that is used inside and outside of a squad car.

This provides officers with a single mobile platform and eliminates the need for multiple devices.

Such a combination of car and tablet or smartphone connectivity can provide camera feeds, results of social media monitoring (especially Twitter, which broadcasts the exact location of a tweeting user), face recognition, license plate scanning results, various record look-ups, building layouts in case of onsite emergencies, gunshot detection results on maps, and many others.

Ideally, such a mobile device should be able to be managed by police officers' verbal commands to free one of their hands. First responders could be equipped with similar functionalities.

- Camera feeds
- Social media listening
- Face recognition
- License plate scanning
- Insurance, driving license, outstanding warrant look-ups
- Building layouts
- Automatic gunshot detection
- Speech recognition

Other digital technologies to protect citizens

Body cameras are already being used to improve police training and better manage community relations as well as to document evidence.

Drones with live video feeds are perfect tools to deploy where spatial real time intelligence is needed and dangerous events are taking place (shootings, explosions, building collapses, etc).

A police robot was used for the first time in Dallas in the summer of 2016 to take down a heavily armed criminal suspected of carrying a bomb and who assassinated several people before he barricaded himself.

Robots are also used to examine suspicious packages, diffuse bombs, and remove hazardous materials.

Police around the country use Twitter to inform and alert the public to ongoing active crimes in their neighborhoods.

And last but not least, with so much information available, it is possible to implement predictive policing based on the extremely successful New York City policing program. It puts historical and current crime data on a map, which allows it to predict the most troublesome spots where crimes are most likely to recur.

To Serve

From a technical perspective, all service interactions with federal and local governments should be digital. Our governments provide mostly services with very little physical component.

Governments deal with a lot of documents, statistics, licenses, permissions, announcements, regulations, inspections, and internal as well as external communication. They accept applications and log complaints and suggestions. All of these activities are perfect candidates for digitization and sharing with the public via well-indexed websites.

All internal government processes are candidates for end-to-end digitization thus making them measurable and more accountable. This includes tax collections, welfare administration, economic development, food inspections, smart transportation, and procurement management, to name a few. Digitization of all documents brings another great benefit, that is, the ability to search for a needle of information in the humongous digital haystack.

- Most interactions between citizens and government should be digital
- All internal government processes should be digitized
- This would lead to more transparency and efficiency

Information sharing

In 2012, the U.S. government has committed to building a 21st Century Government that delivers better digital services to the people. Several major initiatives are focused on providing access to the vast government databases such as census or economic data and making them available via an Application Programming Interface or API.

An API is a standard business software tool used to share data with other applications and systems. It is discussed in depth in Part IV Chapter 8.

Other examples include the Mars Weather API for scientists, the Department of Labor's API for 100 economic indicators, and Arlington National Cemetery's smartphone app to locate gravesites.

- Most government data is public property
- Should be digitized, indexed and easily accessible without special requests

Smart cities

Another aspect of digital government involvement is around delivery and optimization of tangible services. This is especially true for municipal governments leveraging technologies to manage emergencies, traffic, utilities (electricity, water, sewage) and airports.

Smart traffic

Today, major cities have units responsible for managing traffic. Roads, intersections, bridges, and overpasses are equipped with cameras and illumination sensors to monitor real time movement and vibration, as well as dynamic electronic road boards to display traffic signs and instructions.

All the data from all these devices are managed in one place so the traffic unit can coordinate the activities of various agencies involved in traffic issues. They may involve the highway patrol, local sheriff, police, first responders, and radio and TV stations as well as maintenance crews. Most important, intersections and sections of roads and bridges feed live video to large multi-screen panels.

Optimizing traffic and responding to congestion caused by rush hour or emergencies is made possible by this interconnected web of signals, videos, and a live conversation with units on the ground.

In the future, the advent of self-driving technologies will make it possible to include data from vehicles for real-time traffic optimization.

Smart utilities

Many municipalities are also involved in the management of utilities as well as their own buildings. Here digital technologies play a very similar role as in traffic control.

All neuralgic points of an electrical grid and water supply are or should be equipped with sensors measuring the real time flow of electricity or water. Cameras watch the most important nodes. Vibration sensors could facilitate alerts regarding the status of electrical towers and pump engines. Predictive maintenance of expensive equipment would decrease the cost of machine management.

Buildings can be managed by installing smart power meters as well as smart flow meters to optimize heating, AC, energy, and water usage, especially when connected to systems that can selectively take unoccupied spaces out of service.

Here again the same rule applies: the more sensors and the more data, the more effective is the management and optimization of utilities delivery.

Creative applications from local governments include smartphone apps whereby a citizen can take a picture of a problem they encountered, such as uncollected trash, potholes in the streets, abandoned cars, etc, and report it with one click to city hall. The citizen then gets an acknowledgment message and a status report on the action taken.

- Electricity
- Water
- Sewage
- Traffic
- Airports
- Ports

- Smartphone app to report
  - Potholes
  - Trash
  - Abandoned cars
  - Other problems, issues
- Feedback loop

Summary

Citizens are *de facto* customers of local governments. For their taxes and fees they expect an uninterrupted supply of utilities and some relief in traffic. A poor customer experience may lead to a change in the roster of local politicians.

As we discussed before, the general public is used to very high standards of customer experience from private businesses. This puts a lot of pressure directly on governments from the public having high expectations.

Overall, the more data governments share, the more transactions are digital, the more service processes are measured and analyzed, the more transparency, efficiency, and effectiveness will accompany governmental activities.

Like in business, the possibilities for digitization by governments are endless, but challenges are abundant as well. One of the major challenges is the cost of building these information infrastructures. Another is the existence of information silos due to a large number of agencies responsible for distinct functions and keeping records in disjointed systems.

This is a very similar problem to what large businesses face when dealing with disparate data preventing overall analysis of performance.

- Digitization means better protection and service
- Customer experience very relevant
- Services cannot be improved without digitization
- Similar obstacles to digitization to businesses
  - Organizational
  - Budgetary

12
DIGITAL ARCHITECTURE
No Surprises, Please

Imagine that you are in charge of building a new office building for your successful company. The project is estimated at $200 million.

You had several meetings with the architectural team, they provided the final design and now you have to get it approved by the team who is going to spend a lot of time in the new building. In addition to the exterior, everyone would like to see their future offices with windows, furniture, lighting fixtures, conference rooms, the layout of the cafeteria, etc.

This is very hard to do in the traditional way, using blueprints and 2-dimensional pictures. People have a hard time visualizing space, relative height, lighting, etc., even from the best pictures on paper or even 3-dimensional models.

The last thing an architect needs is to have a disappointed client who suffers buyer's remorse after seeing the actual structure in real life and sinking millions of dollars into the project.

Virtual Reality or VR comes to the rescue. All the architectural plans and design details can be digitized and then illustrated in 3D. Now to get approval, you let your customer view the design in almost real surroundings by wearing a VR headset.

Approval is easier and faster, and there are no disappointing surprises when the building is ready to be occupied.

- High stakes
- Hard to visualize
- Many sign-offs involved
- Long process
- No costly surprises

What is also exciting is that an architect can design directly in a VR environment. Instead of drawing things on a flat screen, they can input and try ideas directly in the virtual space.

VR is an example of enhancing the traditional methods of 2-dimensional paper blueprints with 3D design and visualization. It's a completely new digital product that did not exist before, but one that revolutionizes the entire profession.

The benefits are a shorter and cheaper design process, unrestricted creativity leading to better design, happy customers, and as a result, increased chances for another large order and great references.

- Shorter and cheaper design
- Better and more creative design
- Happy customers
- Repeat business

13
DIGITAL CONSTRUCTION AND TRADES

The physical aspect of construction and trade businesses are not likely to change any time soon, if ever. We will always need buildings built, plumbing and HVAC systems installed, appliances connected, walls painted, electricity wired, roofs repaired, yards fertilized, and bugs exterminated.

In this chapter we will concentrate on supporting the functions of construction and the trades.

The single largest challenge in construction is related to the supply chain. Every project is different and the larger the project the more suppliers, parts, workers, and equipment is involved. Every day is a different set of combinations of the above as a project progresses.

Good project management software is a must. It needs to work on smartphones, tablets, and desktops. It has to have superior alerting, reporting, and analysis capabilities. And it needs to be integrated with supply chain data. Otherwise, a multi-million dollar construction project can be severely delayed due to a backordered $10 item.

Updated project status should be as automatic as possible, and any paper input or output processes completely eliminated as they are error prone and not timely. Barcoding, RFID, and smart tags should be used as much as feasible.

In general, the more integration between all possible systems, the better. 3D Building Information Modeling software can be integrated with cost and scheduling for what is referred to as a 5-D approach. This leads to significant savings in cost and time as more interdependencies are discovered and managed sooner rather than later. Some governments, including those in the UK, Finland, and Singapore have mandated the use of these tools for large public projects.

Construction shares a lot of similarities with agriculture from the digitization perspective. It can use drones for documentation of progress on large sites and compile it into 3-D models. Sensors and thermal cameras can help with water management. Connected equipment loaded with various sensors can provide data for better scheduling of regular maintenance plus automatic warnings about any possible malfunctions. As David Wadhwani of AppDynamics said, "A John Deere tractor has more software in it than the Space Shuttle."

In the trades, especially for local businesses offering sales as well as service of the equipment they've sold, the customer experience is extremely important. Communication with customers before, during, and after a job is of the utmost importance. Automatic scheduling, automatic invoicing, automatic reminders about periodic maintenance, and automatic customer satisfaction surveys will minimize the cost of support staff and increase the quality of customer service.

Most trade-based services have pretty good job scheduling software, as this is the core of their business. However, few of these systems are connected to the accounting system in the back end, and the marketing and lead management system in the front end.

Most local trade businesses have similar problems. If they want to make more profit, they have 3 major choices:

1. Increase the number of new customers
2. Sell more to existing customers
3. Streamline operations

In reality, the right combination of the above does the trick. The right combination depends on the type of business, stage of business maturity, competitive conditions, and capital, among others.

Increasing the number of new customers involves getting new leads and turning them into sales. This is easier said than done. Getting new leads could be very expensive. Turning them into sales could be even more costly, especially when long sales cycles and highly paid sales professionals are involved. Getting more sales may not translate to making more money, as you may need to scale up to handle the new business. In summary, you need to get new customers, but it may not immediately translate into more profits.

The much easier and less expensive way to increase profits is to sell more products and services to existing customers. They already trust you and you already know a lot about them. Up-selling and cross-selling are, on average, the best ways to increase profits. There is no cost of customer acquisition and sales processes are already in place. Studies show that increasing customer retention by 5% may lead to the doubling of overall profits.

The third option is to trim costs by streamlining operations. How many manual processes can be eliminated and/or automated? What is the payback time for automation given the initial investment? Here the news is very encouraging, as very inexpensive cloud-based software packages can save a lot of time on repetitive, mundane, manual, and error-prone tasks.

This is especially true in social media activities, email marketing, calendaring, document search, preparation, and management, as well as automated ways to service customers such as scheduling/confirming orders, shipments, deliveries, etc. Another great example here is a dispatch system tied to GPS, as well as a fleet maintenance system for all your vehicles.

Regardless of the combination of the options chosen, one will not increase profits substantially without collecting, analyzing, and reporting more data.

Until recently, it has been very expensive and time consuming to track most activities at a detailed level. Not anymore. The new software packages collect a lot of data automatically and make it easier for analysis and reporting. Thus, increasing profitability has become much easier.

We are breaking a centuries-old vicious circle. We did not collect data because it was too expensive to capture, transmit, and store. We did not analyze data because we did not collect it.

Now, there are no more excuses. Small businesses can now use data to make more money.

14
DIGITAL FINANCIAL SERVICES
Show me the digital money!

Banking should be a pure play digital enterprise. Technically, you do not need to go to the bank at all. You can get cash from your ATM machine without having to interact with a live person.

All cash deposits, transfers, loans, and currency exchanges could be done electronically. There is no technical reason that a bank transfer should take 3 days. There is no technical reason for a mortgage to involve hundreds of paper pages and for the process to take weeks.

With the exception of large and complex commercial loans, there is no reason to involve a banking officer at all. There are political, organizational, and regulatory reasons behind these inefficiencies, but not technical. For example, Walmart failed in its bid to buy a bank.

- Deposits, transfers, loans, currency exchanges
- No technical reason for byzantine mortgage application process
- Political, organizational, and regulatory reasons for lack of more digitization

No single ledger

One of the problems is that there is no single ledger for all banks to clear all its transactions. They have to go through various systems and sometimes even multiple manual processes for a transaction to take effect.
Technically, if all banks in the U.S. (for example) agreed to have a common real time clearing ledger, most transactions would be instant. Today, it's

hard to say when this may happen for the reasons discussed above. Technology exists to accomplish it, but other considerations will have to be addressed before it becomes a reality.

Blockchain and bitcoin are still not mature enough to get the support of all financial institutions, but there will be a growing movement to increase the efficiency of complex and numerous transactions. As of today, I don't feel comfortable predicting when it will happen. I suspect that few people are. I discuss blockchain technologies in Part IV Chapter 8.

Banks compete with each other today on customer experience. This is especially important, as the service they offer is very generic. Thus their websites, mobile apps, online chats, email support, and ease of access to historical transactions are of growing importance.
I myself switched banks only because the former had a very poorly designed interface requiring confusing navigation and many clicks but did not allow me to download detailed historical transactions to Excel.

- No single ledger
- Blockchain and bitcoin not mature enough
- Generic product
- The value of customer experience

Credit Cards

Credit card companies today are a completely pure digital play. They use sophisticated predictive analytics algorithms to discover and prevent fraud, and they support a vast worldwide network of merchants.

Technically, they are a great logistical success spanning the globe, supporting all languages and currencies, and they are a doing relatively good job with customer experience by providing easy access for managing your accounts online. In general, credit card operations are the most advanced financial services companies on the road to digital sophistication.

- Pure digital play
- Spanning the globe
- Connecting most retailers worldwide
- Currency exchange
- Technological marvel
- Good customer experience

Financial Planning – Investments

Financial planning services include the human element of a financial planner and/or tax advisor, mainly trust. They also could be pure digital enterprises using sophisticated algorithms to manage portfolios.

- Human advisor needed due to regulatory and tax complexities
- Trust
- Complex algorithms to manage portfolios

Mobile Payments

There is a big battle brewing about who is going to dominate the smartphone payment market. This fight is among very large players including Apple, Google, Verizon Wireless, Microsoft, and Samsung, as well as PayPal, MasterCard, and Visa.

It remains to be seen what system will dominate the market in the next 5 years. We may be facing a similar situation as we have with credit cards today; i.e., merchants will be accepting few different smartphone payment options.

Again, what is important and relevant is the customer experience. Everything else being equal, the system that ultimately dominates will probably offer the easiest way to transact business for both payees and merchants.

The ideal situation is for payments to be seamless. Imagine a smart cart in a grocery store that tallies all your purchases when you put them inside and then presents you with the total grocery bill to be confirmed with one push of a button (and maybe a pin for security).

There is also an interesting aspect to the security of people who don't carry cash. In underdeveloped countries and some neighborhoods in developed nations, carrying cash on your person is not a good idea. But if your cash is in your phone, even if the phone is stolen or you are robbed, the cash is traceable and thus useless to the thief. So mobile payments lower the risk of doing business that otherwise would be too risky to undertake.

- Apple, Google, Verizon Wireless, Microsoft, Samsung
- PayPal, MasterCard, Visa
- Great potential
  - For dominant player

o   For convenience and safety

Insurance

Insurance is another financial service that could one day be a pure play digital business with no physical agencies or agents. I bought my car insurance, business insurance, home owner insurance, and health insurance online. I wish I could have done so with one vendor or one portal, but nevertheless I did not talk to a live person.

There is an interesting opportunity for property and casualty insurance companies to take advantage of digitally connected sensors. For example, Progressive offers car drivers a discount if they agree to install tracking devices on their cars. These devices track miles driven and can assess the driving style of the insured, thus allowing Progressive to charge premiums based on a custom plan.

The same idea applies to homeowner or renter insurance where sensors connected to the Internet can detect a problem before it becomes costly damage. For example, using temperature sensors attached to pipes, a home monitoring system can detect water leaks.

The idea is very simple: When a tap is running, the pipe will chill. By using the two temperature sensors to detect and measure the temperature differential between the pipe and the ambient temperature, the system can warn owners and tenants of unusual patterns in water usage. Water damage accounts for a quarter of insurance pay-outs on homeowners insurance - much of it in claims caused by small, unnoticed leaks that cause substantial damage over a long period.

The examples above are similar concepts to insurance premium discounts offered for the presence of sprinklers or home security systems. They are just taken a step further by financially and technically feasible sensing and transmission of real-time information.

As for claims processing, some insurance companies already accept pictures of damage taken with smartphones. This saves insurers a costly trip by insurance adjusters.

- Why do we need insurance agents?
- All insurance should be available online
- Custom plans based on behavior or sensors
  - o   Progressive auto policy

- o Water damage insurance
- Remote claim filing

Summary

In summary financial services could be completely digitized and exist with little or no human involvement between a customer and a company. Just like with our credit cards. When was the last time you saw a Visa representative live?

And Visa's risk of doing business with you could be equal or greater than your insurance policy or bank loan. The barriers to complete digitization are not technical. They are related to regulatory limitations.

- Could be completely digitized
- Just like instant worldwide credit card operations
- Barriers to digitization are regulations

15
DIGITAL REAL ESTATE
Still location, location, location

U.S. residential real estate is the nation's single largest physical asset, worth about $26 trillion. The commercial real estate market is of comparable value.

Residential buying

On the residential side, players such as Zillow have made a huge difference in how properties are listed by sellers and found by buyers. Nevertheless, we are still far away from being able to complete the whole residential buying transaction online.

Real estate agents leverage digital marketing, including social media and email; but independent operators face considerable digital marketing competition from the national chains.

Yes, we can search for and find homes using digital applications that include Virtual Reality tours, but few people will make the largest investment of their lives without a physical inspection of their future dwellings.

As discussed in the Financial Services modules, the process of mortgage generation and approval, title search, insurance, and inspections is heavily fragmented and mostly in the hands of local offices not coordinated digitally to provide a single-point, seamless customer experience.

Some of the problems are legal and regulatory; but technically, there is no reason why one should not be able to get one-stop service, accomplishing all the necessary steps digitally. Like in many other industries, what is technically feasible is not possible for other reasons, whether good or bad.

- Searching
- Agent still needed to coordinate
- Few will buy without physical inspection
- Local cottage industries

Residential rental

Airbnb introduced a lot of competition in short term residential rentals, putting more pressure on the hospitality industry as opposed to residential real estate.

It remains to be seen if the Airbnb rental model can be extended to long term residential rentals. It seems to me that renting for over a year involves too much risk without inspecting the dwellings in person. Nevertheless, I can envision an Airbnb service coordinating not only long term rentals but also all the necessary maintenance for landlords *in absentia* by vetting local providers such as plumbers, landscaping, and pest control services, etc.

- Airbnb short term rental disruption
- Service support for *in absentia* landlords?

Commercial

On the commercial real estate side, sites like LoopNet.com or Costar offer functionalities similar to Zillow's for residential properties, with the exception of requiring a subscription fee. The problem is that these and some other sites are not comprehensive and one needs to search multiple sources for a complete list of commercial properties for lease or purchase.

In commercial real estate, it is hard to imagine any large transactions being totally digitized anytime soon. A lot of transactions include extensive analysis of property with respect to allowable usage (such as construction) or negotiations on build-outs on existing properties. In case of very large transactions, a local government may be involved in subsidizing a deal to attract economic development. Such a subsidy may involve tax breaks, or building or fixing roads around the property. Thus, the larger the commercial real estate transaction, the less likely it will ever be completely digitized.

Summary

Both residential and commercial real estate, digital opportunities lie in improving how properties are listed and found. Sound principles of digital marketing are very relevant here. In general, real estate transactions (with the exception of short term residential rentals) are too important to be completed without physical inspections and in-person negotiations, and thus do not lend themselves to a total online shopping experience.

- Search and find only
- Transactions too complex and risky for total digitization
  - Zoning
  - Build-outs
  - Long term incentives

16
DIGITAL AGRICULTURE
Old McDonald Had A Drone

Agriculture is one of the least digitized industries, but the digital potential there is enormous. This is especially true for large operations that can afford to implement technologies that may still be too expensive for smaller farms.

Drones, Sensors, Cameras

Imagine running a farm equipped with weather station measuring current temps, precipitation, humidity, atmospheric pressure, and luminosity. That can use Doppler weather forecast technology.

Using Wi-Fi enabled sensors showing the soil's nitrogen, phosphorous and potassium (N, P, K) content along with pH and soil moisture

In addition you have these inexpensive drones at your disposal. They are equipped with powerful cameras.

An example could be a Red/Green/Blue for visual inspection, elevation modeling, plant counting.

You can also use a Near-infrared cameras for soil property & moisture analysis, crop health/stress analysis, water management, erosion analysis, plant counting

Red-edge cameras could be used for crop health analysis, plant counting, water management.

And last but not least, thermal infrared cameras could be used for plant physiology analysis, irrigation scheduling, maturity evaluation, yield forecasting data from infrared and visual spectrum. These cameras highlight differences between healthy and distressed plants in a way that can't be seen with the naked eye

At your disposal, you also have a fleet of programmable self-driving equipment that can dispense fertilizer or water at desired quantities at specific locations.

Now imagine that all of them are connected with each other in the cloud, and you have the flexibility to place them anywhere, configure, and program to work with each other, and then analyze the results. You do not have to imagine it—farms like this already exist!

In a nutshell, you can identify pests, diseases, and weeds; count plants…

… monitor plant damage and water erosion, plan your harvesting, and, last but not least, optimize irrigation and fertilization as well as application of herbicides and pesticides.

- Sensors, Sensors, Sensors
- Weather forecast
- Irrigation
- Fertilization
- Crop protection
- Harvesting
- Self-driving equipment
- Analytics

Feed the world

It is estimated that the application of such technologies has the potential to improve agricultural productivity up to 30%. In addition, they lead to the optimal use of natural resources, including minimizing the chance of pollution related to unnecessary overuse of agricultural chemicals.

There is a very interesting digital confluence between the agriculture and manufacturing industries. John Deere, as a manufacturer of farm equipment, rolled out the MyJohnDeere.com portal for farmers.

Predictive maintenance and budgeting

At this portal, users can manage the maintenance of their farm equipment. Imagine having 10 pieces of expensive equipment, including tractors. You can enter them all into the system and indicate the future maintenance needs for each piece of equipment. The system will alert you about required oil or belt changes and schedule a visit with a local service center. All the records of all repairs and maintenance are kept on that platform.

Such information is a treasure cove both for the farmer (convenience, reduction in downtime, peace of mind, analysis of ownership costs, among others) and the manufacturer. John Deere gets a lot of information on how and when and in what weather their equipment is being used, and local dealers can better plan warehousing of parts and managing workloads and schedules. It's a win-win-win situation all brought about by better management of information.

- Input all equipment info into a portal
- Budgeting, planning and scheduling maintenance
  - Reduction in downtime
  - Lower cost
- Win-win for farmer and manufacturer

Watch this fascinating video showing the future of digital agriculture.

https://www.youtube.com/watch?v=CYyRryLoQ0w

Agricultural Drone Sensors
https://www.youtube.com/watch?v=SaztuWuDEsg
https://www.youtube.com/watch?v=ikU39yitmYk

Automatic conservation of natural resources
https://vimeo.com/97291773

17
DIGITAL MANUFACTURING

'Manufacturing still has the greatest multiplier effect, in terms
of job creation, of any sector of the economy.'
William Clay Ford, Jr.

Manufacturing is so rich with possibilities that one can write several books just on this subject. Digitization impacts almost all aspects of manufacturing starting with design, quality control, inventory and labor management, utilization of equipment, and sourcing parts and inputs as well as post-sales service.

Major digitization features and benefits

Machines and equipment in manufacturing plants can transmit and receive data over communications networks and can link with analytical systems as well as those belonging to suppliers and distributors.

This means that manufacturers can better monitor how machines and employees are performing and make adjustments to processes. This also leads to better anticipation of machine faults and plans for maintenance programs.

Not all technologies are completely new, but they may be more mature as the same concept can be supported by much more computing power and more granular measurements. For example, we may have been able to monitor the hourly output of injection molding machines. Now, we can monitor, analyze, and optimize the same process on a much more granular level by taking advantage of very detailed data available from electronic controllers that provide information every second on parameters such as temperature, pressure, input quantities, etc.

Final products can also be connected to distributors and buyers and provide information about the way their goods are used, thus shaping future enhancements, customized offerings, and better after-sales service, including warranties. We've touched on this phenomenon already when discussing how John Deere is connected with farmers, owners of their equipment, by MyJohnDeere.com portal.

- All machines transmit & receive data
- All machines connected to
  o Each other
  o Central analytics system
  o Suppliers, distributors & customers
- Process adjustments and optimization
- Predictive maintenance
- Improved sales, service and product design

Major digitization trends in manufacturing

Let's discuss in more depth the major digital trends shaping the following aspects of manufacturing:

- Virtual Design, Virtual Testing, Digital Twin
- 3D Printing
- Advanced Robotics
- Remote monitoring and control
- Optimization of Complex Supply Chain
- Optimization of Production Processes
- Management of Equipment (Asset Management)
- Predictive Maintenance

Virtual Design

Boeing developed airframes for the 777 and 787 using all-virtual design, thus reducing the design time by more than 50 percent. Such reduction has two dimensions; the first is that the design process is less expensive; the second is that it may allow them to get to market quicker than less nimble competitors can. In business, being first with a sustainable innovation can mean a lot.

Modern computer-aided design systems are so capable that one can design extremely complex objects all in the cloud, share ideas, collaborate, and get feedback to the virtual creation without having to build any tangible prototypes.

- Boeing reduces design time by 50%
- Less expensive
- Shorter time to market

Virtual Testing

Companies who manufacture base stations or antennas that manage all voice and data traffic from our smartphones have an interesting testing challenge. How can you test the load of, let's say, 10,000 phones on a given part of your network?

It's hard to imagine that they will get 10,000 physical phones and have them dial at the same time. In addition to phones, they would have to get someone to push the buttons, which would mean engaging about 10,000 testing employees.

Here, again, software came to the rescue. These companies wrote software programs simulating any number of calls being made at the same time and then they hit the antenna with the full load.

Such stress testing would be unthinkable without a virtual set up such as this. On the other hand it would not be advisable to rollout a system that may fail many customers. After all, the customer experience is too important to risk the backlash.

Virtual testing is used in simulating car crashes, too. Instead of crashing real cars, virtual models are subject to crashes at various speeds and results are analyzed. The cost of the test is an order of magnitude less expensive, as real cars are not being used.

Some products are being tested in a hybrid mode. The actual product is tested in a real life environment, but many sensors are placed on it and very granular data is collected centrally to identify problems that would have escaped in less detailed testing.

- Testing cellular tower with 10,000 phones
- Simulated car crashes
- Hybrid approach

- Feasible, shorter, cheaper, more effective

Digital Twin

Here is a textbook definition of a digital twin: "Virtualized design and testing by creating and maintaining a digital representation, or 'digital twin', of any piece of real equipment, and thus of any plant or engine."

Thanks to powerful digital technologies, today we can virtualize design and testing and create a digital representation or "digital twin" of any piece of equipment or plant.

This is huge. In summary, using digital twins for design and testing cuts the cost of prototyping, construction of plants, downtime, and maintenance of machines as well as the cost of failure. This may lead to as much as 20% gains in efficiency. http://gelookahead.economist.com/digital-twin

Digital twin cuts the cost of
- prototyping (design and testing)
- construction
- downtime
- failure
- maintenance

3D Printing or Additive Manufacturing

3D printing is a bit of a misnomer. I prefer 'additive manufacturing' as it better reflects the nature of the process. However, 3D printing has already become a household term, so let's keep using it.

Let's say you want to create a simple cylindrical vase for your flowers. Let's assume that you already have a software file representing the desired 3D shape.

You load this file into your computer, connect your 3D printer, send a 'Print' command, and wait for the printer to create this vase from plastic, ceramics, or metal.

The process is quite simple. Let's assume we will be using plastic. The 3D printing software virtually 'sliced' your vase into thousands of horizontal layers.

Next, the printer starts spraying one 'slice' or layer on top of each other the moment the previous layer is dry. So, the printer actually builds up your vase gradually from the bottom up, slice by slice. Think salami slicing and putting it back together by stacking slices on top of each other.

This concept has been around for the last 30 years, but the printers were too expensive, computers too weak, and software neither powerful nor friendly to use. Now you can have a simple 3D printer for a couple hundred dollars. Industrial printers are in the range of thousands of dollars.

You are not limited to plastic as far as your material. You can use metals including gold and silver. You can even use ceramics.

- Software slices your 3D design to thousands of layers
- Liquid hot plastic gets sprayed on a flat surface in the shape of the first layer
- When the first layer is solid, the next gets sprayed on top of it
- Vase is gradually built from ground up
- Plastic, ceramics and metals including gold and silver

One part at a time

You can cheaply create a single copy of a desired object for prototyping and testing, thus speeding up the process and making it less expensive and more transparent.

You can recreate individual parts for products that have been discontinued. Think spare parts for antique cars.

Instead of warehousing parts that are not in high demand, you produce them one at a time, only when needed. This helps to reduce the cost of warehousing of rarely used parts.

You can create one-off custom products such as metal jewelry or parts for hearing aids that reflect the shape of your inner ear, or custom prosthetics.

- Single copy of a product for prototyping
  - Less expensive design
  - Shorter time to market
- Recreate parts for discontinued products
- Decrease warehousing cost by producing rarely purchased items
- Create custom shapes such as hearing aids or prosthetics

The future of 3D printing

Is 3D printing going to replace traditional manufacturing methods like injection molding or metal machining? The answer depends on the confluence of the cost of printers and their speeds as well as the cost of liquefying large quantities of metal or ceramic materials.

However, today, for example, 96 percent of custom-made hearing aids in the world are created by 3D printers.

Some fascinating medical 3D printing applications are discussed in the Digital Healthcare section.

- 3D printing is a slow process
- Can it replace traditional methods?
- 96% of custom made hearing aids in the world are 3D printed
- Application in medicine

Large Robots

Between 1999 and 2014, orders for industrial robots almost doubled to 20,000 units. According to the *PwC MoneyTree Report*, capital investment in industrial robots by U.S. ventures rose to about $172 million in 2013, nearly tripling 2011 levels.

Around 70% of all robots in North America were deployed in the automotive industry, mostly for machining and assembly. Traditional robots tend to be very large.

- Orders for robots doubled between 1999 and 2014
- Between 2011 and 2013, investment in robots tripled
- 70% of robots are used in automotive industry
- Very large - hard to relocate

Smaller, portable robots

The new ones are lighter and more portable, allowing for shorter runs of niche products without a lot of effort on reconfiguring factories. New robots have more sensors and are easier to configure.

The new generation of robots can perform finer and more precise tasks such as assembling consumer-electronics items or even sewing garments. As robots get less expensive, easier to set up, and more functional, they can reduce labor force cost so much that the U.S. and other high-wage economies may be able to recover manufacturing business previously off-shored to China, Mexico, and other low labor cost countries.

As robots get cheaper and more 'intelligent' due to the increased capabilities of sensors and artificial intelligence, they will pick up some other mundane tasks such as packaging, slicing, and preparing food.

There are obvious applications for robots in the military and for disaster recovery. After all, it's better to lose a robot than to risk a human life.

There is considerable anticipation that robots may even help with household chores in the future, like Rumba is helping with vacuuming today. This may help the elderly population to live independent lives.

- Lighter, portable and easier to configure
- Smaller, more precise tasks
  o Packaging
  o Slicing
  o Sewing
  o Preparing food
  o Military/police assistance
  o Disaster recovery
- Competitive impact - can reduce labor cost
- Elderly care - household chores

Sensors, sensors, sensors

In general, robots depend on the interaction of many sensors, software, hardware, and telecommunications technologies.

They are the ultimate transparent and accountable employees, productive, precise, with an audit trail of all performed tasks, never tired, and never asking for a raise. :-)

Robots may someday play a significant role in solving labor shortage problems in developed countries. This may reduce the competitive advantage now held by low labor cost countries.

Related to that is the common problem of all aging societies. Can we use future robots to take care of household chores for the elderly so they can stay independent in their households as long as possible? If we combine it with telemedicine, I can see a great potential!

- Functionality function of
  - Software
  - Sensors
  - Telecommunication
- Ultimate employees
  - Precise
  - Never tired
  - Always right
  - Never asking for a raise :-)
- Potential in solving labor shortage
- Potential in elderly care

Remote monitoring and control

Digital monitoring brings new capabilities and unprecedented access to process monitoring and control. Using standard process sensors, such as temperature, pressure, flow, or other sensors, you can monitor, control, or log data from anywhere around the world.

With the right setup and configuration, you will know that your process, no matter how large, is functioning optimally. If it does not, you will be notified by text, call, or email. No news means good news.

This peace of mind is not possible today, as you do not know *what you do not know*.

In addition, all the data will be logged and accessible to you anywhere based on the need to know. So if you want to diagnose a problem you just learned about, you can access your analytics anywhere.

- Unprecedented access to monitoring and control
- Connected sensors + smartphone = 24/7 monitoring and control
- Before you did not know what you didn't know
- Peace of mind
- Logs and audit trail

Facility Management

Imagine you are in charge of monitoring a large manufacturing plant. You need to monitor the temperature, humidity, dew point, and lighting. No problem—there are sensors for that.

There are also sensors that would alert you to an open door, broken window, or sprinklers going off. You can have a simple web-enabled camera so you can view the scene right on your computer.

At night, you may want to turn on your motion detector sensors and a corresponding farm of drones. When an undesirable motion is detected, a drone dispatches itself and starts streaming video of the affected area.

When you see a crime in progress, you just call the local police or your security team. This may sound like science fiction, but motion sensors and drones are much less expensive than hiring a large security team.

- Managing a large warehouse
  - Temperature, humidity, dew point
  - Door open, window broken, sprinkler went off
  - Web cam inside and out
  - Motion sensor on the perimeter
  - Drone farm with cameras
- Lower cost, increased effectiveness due to shorter reaction time

Optimization - Production Processes

We have just demonstrated that we can monitor and control almost any manufacturing process. The limitations seem to be financial, not technical.

Today, there are sensors on almost anything that is relevant to production and security. However, not all the steps in the process may be worth monitoring, or you may just not have the budget for it and have to take a chance, or do it the old fashioned way by walking around.

- Limits to monitoring is financial not technical
- Not everything is worth measuring and monitoring

Sufficient granularity and frequency affords optimization

If you can monitor and control remotely with the right granularity and frequency, you can *start* optimizing. As we mentioned before, the fact that we monitor and control does not mean that our processes are optimal with respect to the final outcome.

As an example, consider pumping water out of a lake or river for the municipal water supply. We can monitor how many gallons we pumped and we can stop the pumping if we get enough water in the tanks.

The question is whether we pumped the water the most economical way. Pumping very slowly may suffice, and we can use cheaper pumps. If we want to replenish water quickly, we may need more powerful, hence expensive, pumps.

We may run them on variable speeds depending on the demand. There is a trade-off between the speed of pumping and the price of pumping. Maybe we only pump water at night, when electricity is cheaper.

Depending on the requirements, we may use algorithms to optimize the process as we have all the necessary inputs. This is a pretty simple example to make a point, but imagine a complex process made up of many interlocking steps, such as power plant operations.

Without the right algorithms, we have a 100% chance that our process is not optimal and hence too expensive.

- Perfect monitoring and control does not mean optimization
- The outcome maybe pumping x gallons of water
- The better outcome is to pump it as cheap and as fast/slow as possible

Management of equipment

Imagine again that you run a very large manufacturing facility. You can monitor the things we discussed in the previous section, but do you know where all your equipment is?

For larger, mobile items you may use GPS devices to keep track of them. For smaller items, you may want to attach an RFID chip to the equipment so when it's being moved around you can keep track of it with RFID readers.

RFIDs are also great for managing the movement of small equipment and parts to and from the warehouse. With the right procedures and enough RFID readers, you could know at any time where the thousands of pieces of your equipment or parts are.

You need to make sure that your operators have instant access to this information via tablets or smartphones in case of emergencies and unexpected contingencies as production processes are not 100% predictable.

More detailed RFID discussion can be found in Part IV, Chapter 9.

- Where is your equipment?
- GPS
- RFID chips

Predictive maintenance

OK, so we know where our equipment is. But do we know when we have to service complex equipment made of many parts that may require maintenance at different intervals?

Just like our cars, it's different for an oil change versus wheel alignment versus AC service. With one or two cars, it's very easy. But what if you have hundreds of trucks, cars, a couple of planes, and a dozen large Caterpillars, and each type of equipment requires different timeframes for inspections and service?

The only way to effectively manage such complexity is to input all equipment as well as their serviceable parts into a software program and tag each part with the date of the upcoming service and the description of such service.

This will enable you to create a schedule of required service or replacement for all the parts for all your equipment. What is the benefit of that?

GREG GUTKOWSKI

You can plan your budget as these services come at a cost. You can plan when you need to buy them or schedule a service. You don't want to do it at the last minute, risking interruption of your production process.

- When do you need to service your equipment?
- Input all equipment and parts in software platform
- Tag each equipment/part with time, duration and cost of service
- Minimize downtime due to timely service
- Estimate budget
- Plan and schedule maintenance

Predicting failure

So far, we have just discussed how to account for all the assets and have them serviced based on the manufacturers' specs. The next step is whether we can predict failure of any of these parts. Manufacturer specs are usually based on average usage, and we may be working our equipment very hard. We cannot risk interrupting production based on unexpected equipment failures.

IoT (Internet of Things concept is discussed in Part IV, Chapter2) types of solutions are used to solve this problem. Here is an example of predicting the failure of a large electric engine powering a water pump.

One simple Wi-Fi enabled vibration sensor is attached to the top of the engine. One simple Wi-Fi power meter measures the input of energy.

We already have a flow meter installed, so we know how much water is being pumped. Therefore, in real time we know how much energy is being used, how much water is being pumped, and how severe the vibrations are.

All this data is in the cloud and processed by analytical software. If the vibration level exceeds certain limits and the engine takes too much energy for the same unit of water pumping, we know we may have a problem and we can send a text warning to the operator on this shift.

This information may be priceless or irrelevant. Everything depends on the importance of this engine being operational to your business objectives. If you can wait 2 days with an engine not working, it's not worth measuring it. If you can lose several millions of dollars due to a 2-hour interruption, then it would make sense to spend $1,000 to monitor it.

- Combination of sensors and power usage

- Vibration, corrosion, leakage

Digital Manufacturing Summary

We have discussed that manufacturing is rife with digital improvement opportunities. The ultimate potential is total automation of production processes. This has a profound impact on labor cost, labor relations, required skills, and quality of life. Whatever we track, we can control, optimize, and then automate.

The situation in manufacturing is similar to agriculture: A lot of moving parts, large spaces, collaboration with a multitude of suppliers and distributors, as well as operations ranging from rather small to very large being managed by family members or professional managers.

From the perspective of a top manufacturing executive, the relevant question is how to allocate budgets, energies, and talents among various digital initiatives. In other words, where is the lowest hanging digital fruit and what does it take to harvest it?

Because the digital revolution is very new and technologies are changing very fast, there are just not enough executives with the relevant experience. As a result, the adoption of even the best concepts may be delayed until that knowledge reaches decision makers. This is not limited to manufacturing. It's an issue for all businesses and organizations.

- Lots of potential - up to total automation
- Lot of complexity
- Limits in adoption are structural and financial, not technical
- Limited executive experience on how to allocate digital energies among
  - Increasing revenue
  - Tightening up and optimizing existing processes
  - Introducing new digital products/services

Watch these videos on virtual design and testing

Boeing 737-800 Virtual Design
https://www.youtube.com/watch?v=vbN7tXYL7gA

Simulated car crash

https://www.youtube.com/watch?v=jAOUrsnt8CA

For a visual representation of various 3D printing possibilities, watch the following videos:

3D printing fun
https://www.youtube.com/watch?v=4OfRD5bfJWA

Get started with 3D printers
https://www.youtube.com/watch?v=ZIPYMdxw4qU

The 2015 DARPA Robotics Challenge Finals
https://www.youtube.com/watch?v=8P9geWwi9e0

Robotics and 3D printing. This video shows the combination of 3D and robotic technologies
https://vimeo.com/117134365

The Highly Biomimetic Anthropomorphic Robotic Hand
https://vimeo.com/154571244

Recommended Reading
http://www.pwc.com/us/en/industrial-products/next-manufacturing/robotics-rise-of-robots.html
http://www.mckinsey.com/business-functions/operations/our-insights/manufacturings-next-act

http://www.mckinsey.com/business-functions/operations/our-insights/digital-manufacturing-the-revolution-will-be-virtualized

18
DIGITAL NON PROFITS
Please give digitally

Most nonprofits face a challenge similar to the media and PR industries. They compete for the attention span of many donors who have a lot of options and opinions.

Most non-profits offer a variety of services as opposed to manufacturing or producing something.

Most non-profits are also highly dependent on the trust of their donors, so they need to make their presence and activities as transparent as possible to the public, including their evaluations posted on sites such as GuideStar.

The more non-profits depend on individual contributions as opposed to corporate sponsorships, the more they are dependent on superior digital marketing. Their website presence, email campaigns, social media activities, and paid advertising have to be very well designed, coordinated, and managed.

- Mostly intangible services
- Dependent on trust of donors
- Dependent on superior digital marketing
    - Website
    - Social media
    - Email
    - Online ads

- Digital donations made easy
  - o Smartphone based
  - o Recurring donations

- Crowd funding

If their activities also include services such as housing, distribution of food or other goods, or assistance with medical and transportation needs, they are subject to the same trends described in previous chapters. For example, if a charity is distributing food to needy individuals around a large city or area, it may greatly benefit from the optimization of their delivery fleet equipped with GPS (like any other logistical operation).

Most smaller non-profits face problems similar to small businesses. They cannot afford to attract the right talent, neither are they effective in retaining it even if they can afford to hire it.

Therefore, we see a lot of cooperation among smaller non-profits with independent digital marketing agencies.

Given a small staff wearing multiple hats, it is very important to digitize and optimize internal processes.

- When providing tangible benefits - logistics and transportation challenges
- When small, it's hard to attract and retain digital marketing talent
- Need to optimize internal office processes

19
DIGITAL MILITARY
If you want peace, digitize

The U.S. military can take advantage of all the benefits of the digital revolution. Actually, it frequently leads the effort. Over the years, many military digital inventions ended up in civilian products:

Research and Development Lab

The U.S. military is a great digital R&D lab for the whole society and has had a profound impact on both the digital revolution and the GDP of the United States. DARPA is leading these efforts. DARPA stands for the Defense Advanced Research Project Agency. It is an agency of the U.S. Department of Defense responsible for the development of emerging technologies.

This is not a new trend of military leading the way; canned food was invented by the military to get unspoiled food to soldiers during the Civil War. So were the containers used to solve the complexity of shipping military equipment all over the globe.

First of all, the Internet itself was built by the military to manage a possible atomic attack by the Soviet Union. Other examples include, lasers, GPS, databases (Oracle was first built for the CIA), motion sensors, computer mouse, on-screen windowing (a precursor to Windows and Apple interfaces), interactive computer maps (a precursor to Google and Apple maps), voice recognition (a Siri enabler), the Unix computer operating system, chemical and biological sensors, satellite communication and environmental monitoring from space sensors, autopilot systems on passenger planes, drones, and microwave ovens, to name a few.

- Internet
- Laser
- GPS
- Databases
- Motion sensors
- Computer mouse
- Windows as computer interface
- Computer maps
- Voice recognition
- Satellites
- Unix operating system
- Drones
- Microwave ovens

The next frontier

There is the reasons why we are discussing the military at the end of our discussion of various industrial sectors. If not already contributing to many of them, the military can leverage all of them. For example, all technologies available to police as described in the Digital Government section are also applicable to the military.

Artificial intelligence, drones, robotics, motion sensors, etc. have a perfect place in the military. Actually, they have great potential to save our soldiers' lives as more and more operations can be completed without having troops on the ground. Public and political support for the military is always inversely related to the number of our casualties.

In particular, a combination of drones, robots, pattern recognition, and GPS guided missiles are very promising in the future of warfare. These capabilities combined with sophisticated communication will be very hard to match by any army, especially from less developed countries, our most likely adversaries.

All medical digital achievements can help our veterans, especially robotic prosthetics and 3D printing of custom implants.

Digital marketing helps in recruiting and public relations. This includes attracting the brightest technological minds to collaborate with DARPA.

Digital improvements in logistics are highly relevant as well. After all, shipping containers were invented by the military to solve problems with moving a lot of equipment all over the world. Wars are won by having better information and better logistics. Napoleon and Hitler got a sobering appreciation for the latter while trying to conquer the vast lands of Russia.

Even more and better entertainment and education can be provided to soldiers in more locations and on their schedules by streaming it to various devices.

The Military, like all other industrial sectors, has organizational constraints, and not necessarily technological limitations. What is feasible technologically is not always possible, either financially or politically.

A digital marvel

Nevertheless, the U.S. military is a digital marvel spanning the whole globe. The combination of the naval fleet, army troops, and airborne forces spread over 7 continents, connected by a vast web of satellites and supported by a network of powerful databases, gives the United States unmatched capabilities throughout the world.

One can say that the United States owes its world military dominance in big part to the country's digital superiority. A logical extension of this finding is that we ultimately owe our freedoms to the digital accomplishments. Our allies also enjoy their freedoms due to the protective U.S. digital might.

It's worth noting that a lot of technology companies welcome veterans to their ranks upon decommission from the military. Where else could they find so many digital skills combined with maturity and high motivation?

- 7 Continents
- Navy
- Army
- Air Force
- Marines
- National Guard
- Veterans

20
DIGITAL MATURITY
How industries compare

In this chapter, we will discuss how various industries compare to each other with respect to their digital maturity or how well they take advantage of the digital revolution.

According to the McKinsey study* following is the ranking of the relative digital maturity of various industries in the U.S.

1. ICT
2. Media
3. Professional Services
4. Finance and Insurance
5. Wholesale trade
6. Advanced manufacturing
7. Oil and gas
8. Utilities
9. Chemicals
10. Basic goods manufacturing
11. Mining
12. Real estate
13. Transportation
14. Education
15. Retail
16. Entertainment and recreation
17. Personal and local services
18. Government
19. Healthcare

20. Hospitality
21. Construction
22. Agriculture

As expected, Information and Communication Technologies (ICT) and Media lead the pack.

The least digitized sectors are Government, Healthcare, Hospitality, Construction, and Agriculture.

This ranking supports our hypothesis that it is not the lack of technology that separates digitally mature industries from the less mature. After all, digital technologies are available to all. It's more about the financial and organizational boundaries that may be in the way.

For example, the hospitality industry is made up of many small operators who may not have the economies of scale to take advantage of all the available tools, as opposed to large, heavily concentrated media companies who can spread out the cost of digitization. The same may be true with construction and agriculture.

In government and healthcare, organizational issues are slowing the digitization process. Between control and funding issues and the lack of a market mechanism, there is less incentive to digitize despite favorable economies of scale.

*http://www.mckinsey.com/industries/infrastructure/our-insights/imagining-constructions-digital-future

PART III
DIGITIZING EXISTING BUSINESS PROCESSES

1
INTRODUCTION
Digitize Now, Play Later

Not all industries or companies were disrupted by the digital revolution. Businesses with a physical component such as agriculture, manufacturing, construction, or even local dentists, for example, are not going to be disrupted by the Uber or Amazon business models.

Nevertheless, all business processes in all industries are greatly impacted by digitization. In this part, we will discuss the impact of digitization on common business processes in every industry.

First, we will discuss the benefits, complexity, and cost associated with measuring processes. This will be followed by a detailed discussion of the impact of the digital revolution on common business processes.

Benefits of process digitization

There are several major advantages to process digitization in general:

- The first is that a digitized process is more easily traceable and measurable, thus more transparent and accountable. As the old adage says, 'If you cannot measure, you cannot manage'.

- The second is that a digitized process can be automated and thus made less expensive by the elimination of expensive labor and manual mistakes. You simply cannot automate a process if you don't measure it.

- The third is the feasibility of optimization, which guarantees that a process is the most effective and efficient it can be. Automation by itself does not guarantee that the process is the most efficient or effective. At the same time, it is easier to optimize a process if it is automated.

- The fourth is the ability to benchmark processes across in the same industry to compare similar processes to collectively learn what works the best.

Benchmarking is very good way to assess if a given process meets the standard within an industry. Such information may be used for the actual process management as well as part of the valuation of a company when it's time for sale. Everything else being equal, a company with much more efficient processes will command a higher sale price.

- Traceable - if you cannot measure, you cannot manage or improve
- Automation
- Optimization
- Benchmarking

Benefits of detailed process measurement

Today, every business process should start and stop on a digital device (smartphone, tablet, laptop, desktop, sensor) even if it has a heavy physical component. If it does not, it is very hard to measure and thus automate, optimize, and benchmark.

When we put a time and name stamp on every required step of a process, we can measure its basic statistics. This includes overall process duration, time on task for each step, quantities of resources required, approvals, etc.

This allows for automatic notification to the right person about missing information or input for each step, or process completion. Internal standards can be set for the duration of the process and this can lead to the identification of bottlenecks, training needs, or process modifications, especially if we combine cost data with it.

- Every process should start and stop digitally even if it includes manual steps
- Process duration
- Time on task
- Approvals

- Alerts
- Standards
- Bottleneck identification

Today's $200K mortgage application process

Imagine managing a long, complex process involving multiple individuals in multiple locations doing most of their work by hand. What you have, for example, is the nightmare of today's mortgage application process. It's hard to know at any given moment who is waiting for whom and for how long and why.

Let's imagine a couple buying their first home, anxiously awaiting approval of their $200K mortgage. The process can be stuck due to either the real estate agent, home inspector, insurance agent, title clerk, or a banker who are all in separate physical locations and work for different institutions that have different incentives for employee performance.

Our poor applicants have no idea where things are and how long the process will last. At the end of that adventure, they are supposed to manually sign hundreds of pages of paper.

At the same time, I can wire $200K from my bank to another financial institution entering only my username, password, and a verification code displayed on my smartphone. In both cases, the transaction amount is $200K, so the risks are comparable.

- Multiple individuals involved at multiple locations
  - o It's hard to know who is waiting for whom
  - o Real estate agent?
  - o Home inspector?
  - o Insurance agent?
  - o Title clerk?
  - o Loan officer?
- Hundreds of pages, hundreds of signatures
- Takes days, even weeks
- Anxiety, poor customer experience, waste of time and energy
- But can wire $200K in seconds

Complexity of some processes

Other examples of complex processes exist in manufacturing, which may require coordination of multiple global suppliers, shipments, production lines, and quality control checks. It is not uncommon for a complex product like a car to be made up of over 500 parts coming from 50 different suppliers in 5 different countries.

- Complexity of managing multiple
  - o Parts
  - o Suppliers
  - o Shipments
  - o Assembly lines
  - o Warehouses
  - o Quality checks, etc

Cost of measurement

Tracking processes have always had some costs associated with it. It may be the cost of inspection, cost of manual input, the price of sensors or meters, or data transmission as well as the cost of professional time spent on analysis. Nevertheless, the general trend is that software, telecommunications, and hardware costs are only going down and at some point, almost every major process should be audited for the economics of the measurement.

An oil gauge on my $30K car engine costs about $200 dollars, so it makes perfect sense to spend $200 to protect $30K investment. The situation would be very different if the oil gauge cost $10K. Would it be worth the measuring oil level then? There are no easy answers—every process needs to be evaluated separately in the context of the overall business context.

In other words, however elegant the plan, one should occasionally look at the results.

- Inspection
- Manual input
- Price of meters
- Data transmission
- Time spent on analysis
- Would you spend $10,000 to track $30,000 processes?

2
HUMAN RESOURCES

'My men are my money'
Amit Kalantri

Let's examine the first process - recruitment. In hiring, web-based job boards, LinkedIn, document scanning and OCR (Optical Character Recognition), background and reference checks, scheduling interviews, approvals, and all correspondence could be all digital and mostly automated.

Today, for example, many organizations accept and even encourage applying for a job with a LinkedIn profile. It makes the process more efficient and transparent. No more scanning and less resume padding as it is harder to do when a document is open to public scrutiny.
We expect this trend to continue and thrive since Microsoft acquired LinkedIn. Microsoft already has a prominent presence in corporate America and it can position LinkedIn as a great process improvement for HR departments.

- Job boards
- LinkedIn
- Scanning
- Optical Character Recognition - OCR
- Reference checks
- Scheduling meetings
- Approvals
- Correspondence

The overall effect of digitizing hiring processes is the lower cost of recruiting, better communication with hiring managers, and better communication with highly desirable candidates who may have multiple job offers.

The top metrics for recruiting are time to fill, time to hire, qualified candidates per hire, and interview per hire. They seem simple, but without a process that accounts for every step, they may be very hard to compile, trust, and use.

- Lower cost of recruiting
- Better quality candidates
- Better quality of employees
- Simple metrics but very hard to manage without digitization

Professional Development

Most professional development today is already based on extensive libraries of self-paced online training courses. Given that all professions need a lot of continuing education, and the high cost of instructor-led courses, self-paced online training is going to become a staple of professional education.

We can measure the number and type of courses taken, time on task, and completion rates, and thus try to understand the relationship between the amount and type of training offered and expected business outcomes.

Today, for most organizations it's rather hard to measure the effectiveness of professional development despite the considerable effort tied to this activity.

- Online courses
- Courses taken
- Time on task
- Completion rates
- Hard to measure effectiveness without digitization

The future

The task of managing applicant flow through the hiring process is relatively easy to automate and analyze. There are several good software packages on the market that already do that.

The greater challenge lies in digitizing the process of identifying the always-changing set of relevant skills and identifying the right talents, so as to attract the best candidates and retain them.

I see HR departments slowly evolving toward a high value add function as described above. Today, many HR departments focus mainly on keeping the tort lawyers as far away as possible.

In order to accomplish such an ambitious task, HR departments will have to better understand the digital transformation in the context of their own business. Otherwise, it will be hard to assess the skills to be attracted and nourished without broad knowledge of internal processes, products, services, and markets.

If it is true that employees are the company's greatest asset, then we will have to treat employees with the same reverence as we extend to our most valuable customers. Otherwise, unhappy with their 'internal customer experience', they will walk into the waiting arms of the competition or start a competing business. So, everything we discussed with respect to 'customer experience' is also relevant to the employee experience.

Thus, we need to rethink how we even list our jobs and how to facilitate the best match between our needs and candidate characteristics and preferences. Making such a match on keywords on resumes may not be sufficient anymore. Today, on average, recruiters spend only 8 seconds per resume, fetched for them by a keyword matching algorithm. It does not seem like an effective way to source the best talent.

In the near future, assessing skills in just a few seconds and making a match with a vague job description is not going to be sufficient. Moreover, we need to assess candidates' values, interests, motivations, communication styles, hobbies, and preferences.

This cannot be done by a simple match of keywords between the job description and a resume. Nor can it be done effectively on a large scale via personal interviews. First, it would be too time consuming. Second, we would need for every interviewer to have PhD-level knowledge about the human psyche.

The answer is to include in-depth psychological and skill assessment on each candidate and then match them to available opportunities that are described in a broad context. Easier said than done; however, digital technologies come to the rescue again.

There a several reputable vendors offering online tools for comprehensive and reliable psychological and skills assessments. The trick is to take their output and match it with a well written job description that includes relevant psychological, technical, and physical requirements.

The same assessment technologies can be used on an ongoing basis as skills, jobs, and interests change over time.

Then, it becomes a technical problem that can be solved with technology. However, no technology will solve this problem if the right skills, aptitudes, and attitudes are not identified on both sides of the equation.

The same assessment technologies also become a great way to identify and match professional development training and resources.

The potential for benefits of better employee-employer match-making are enormous and numerous:

- Lower cost of hiring
- Lower cost of on-boarding
- Lower cost of training
- Lower cost of retaining
- Better education
- Better skills
- Higher motivation
- Higher performance
- Higher retention
- Desirable workplace
- 5 Stars on Glassdoor.com (making attracting top talent even easier

3
MARKETING

'The best marketing doesn't feel like marketing.'
Tom Fishburne

Off all the existing business processes, marketing is the one most impacted by recent digitization—by digital pay-per-click advertising, Search Engine Optimization (SEO or ranking in Google and other search engines), social media, advanced email capabilities, powerful databases, sophisticated websites, and complex analytics.

- Pay-Per-Click
- Search Engine Optimization - SEO
- Social Media
- Email Marketing
- Sophisticated Websites
- Complex Analytics

The traditional definition of marketing is still relevant. It includes coordination of the 4 Ps:

- Product - development of a product
- Price - setting its price
- Place - selection of place to reach customers
- Promotions - development and implementation of promotions

Digital marketing is nothing more than using digital technologies to manage the four Ps. These technologies are relevant to all four of them. For example, a new product could be an iPhone app, pricing could be dynamic based on real time auctions like prices for Google ads, distribution may be through an e-commerce store, and promotion may take the form of a paid advertisement on Facebook.

This does not mean that the digital ways are at the exclusion of traditional ones. On the contrary, they should work and support each other. E-commerce sites may coexist with a network of traditional distributors. Paid advertising on Google does not exclude promoting businesses during traditional trade shows. Posting on social networks can complement a handwritten "thank you" note.

Digital Marketing

As described below, a digital marketing framework is based on your website and four digital channels supporting traditional marketing:

- Website
- Search
- Email
- Paid ads
- Social media

Website – Pull

Your website is the heart of your Internet presence. A good website has the following attributes:

1. Informs about your products and company
2. Is easy to use
3. Can easily be found when your products are searched on the Internet (attracts the right visitors and pulls them in)
4. Converts visitors to prospects or customers (by calling or filling out a form)
5. Collects as many email addresses as possible from visitors
6. Makes money for you (in the case of e-commerce sites)

Most websites today exhibit only the first attribute. They are nice electronic business cards collecting digital dust because few can be found.

- Informs
- Is easy to use
- Is easily found

- Converts visitors to prospects or customers
- Collects email addresses
- Makes money

Search – Pull

You need to be found easily on the Internet when a prospective customer is looking for your product. You need to pull your prospects to your website. There is a set of techniques called Search Engine Optimization, or SEO, to accomplish that goal. They are based on the concept of matching what a prospective customer types into Google with what is described on your website.

For example, if a prospective customer enters "shower door manufacturer" in a Google search, and you are in the shower door business, it would be desirable for your website to be listed on the first page of results.

Very few people go to the 2nd page of Google when searching, hence there's a lot of competition to be on the first page, especially on smartphones.

- Need to be easily found
- Search Engine Optimization
- Matching what's being sought with what's on your website
- The best place to hide a dead body is on the second page of Google search results

Email – Push

Email is a great way to stay in touch with existing customers and prospects that shared their email address with you on your website. Email does not get much media attention, but it's a very effective and very inexpensive way to push your message out on a periodic basis.

- Great to communicate with existing customers
- Very effective and inexpensive
-

Paid Ads – Push and Pull

Paid ads may be displayed when a prospect is searching for you in Google – this is a form of a "pull." However, paid ads can also be displayed when prospects are visiting media sites and your product is complementary to the theme of an article they read. For example, when someone is reading about air quality, an ad about clear air monitoring equipment is "pushed" next to the article.

- Pushing the message out
- Pulling the prospects in

Social Media – Push and Pull

Social media serves a dual role as far as pulling and pushing your message out. You may be posting and pushing messages on many social media sites in order to pull some visitors to your own social media site or blog. It is very hard to measure the impact of social media on revenues.

- Pushing the message out
- Pulling the prospects in
- Hard to measure effectiveness

Digital Glue

The digital marketing framework is glued together by relevant and consistent content flowing among all the channels doing the pushing and pulling. We need to assure conceptual as well as graphical consistency on all fronts of our Internet presence.

The digital currency of Internet marketing includes specific keywords describing your products and services. These keywords have to be present on your website, and in your emails, social media posts, and paid ads.

- Consistent content on all channels
- Keywords are the currency of digital marketing

Whether you are looking for new distributors or direct buyers of large items, your website must stand up to close examination. Buyers will take the first steps to do due diligence on your business. If they land on a hard-to-use site with little relevant information, the likelihood of getting them engaged goes to zero.

Thus, you face two challenges. The first one is to be found by tuning your website to the buying signals. The second is to keep your visitor engaged after they've found you. The best way to achieve the second objective is to provide as much information in a relevant format in as few clicks as possible by having a fast loading site (i.e., fact sheets, videos, PDF downloads, testimonials, and contact details).

- Establishing credibility
- Keeping visitors engaged

Traditional Marketing Turbocharged

In just the last 10 years, traditional promotional strategies had to be either replaced or turbocharged with their digital equivalents. Print and TV advertising yielded to online ads and YouTube videos, ranking in Google was not even part of marketing mix, neither were social media.

Few marketers had to pay attention to the technical details of their websites and even fewer were involved in complex analysis of web traffic. Now, these capabilities are a must.

Today, you can find a finance manager with 25 years of experience in their field, but you cannot find a digital marketing manager with more than 6 to 7 years of experience in the digital world.

In addition, digital marketing involves a multitude of skills such as graphic design, copywriting (ranking in Google requires a lot of good writing on your website,) video production, photography, email marketing, and social media expertise as well as website ranking (SEO) proficiency. This has to be supported by the highly technical skills of website security and database implementation, integral parts of most websites today.

- Relatively new tools
- SEO and Social Media were not in the mix just 10 years ago
- Technical details - not a traditional marketing skill
    - Graphic designers
    - Copywriters
    - Video producers
    - Email marketing experts
    - SEO specialists
    - Pay-per-click managers

Digital Marketing Skills Gap

Never before has marketing involved such a wide variety of skills from creative to highly technical and analytical. Analytical skills especially are in short supply as universities do not [yet] widely offer a lot of analytics-based curricula and there are not a lot of opportunities to train on the job.

This lack of experienced managers plus the wide variety of skills required to run an effective digital promotional campaign leads many companies to partner with digital marketing agencies who are better positioned to manage such a diverse range of talents.

This is especially true for smaller businesses who cannot afford to have full time positions for each of these functions. Even if they could afford to hire them, they would have a problem retaining such talent, which usually thrives on a constant variety of assignments.

- Wide variety of skills required
- Creative & analytical
- Smaller businesses have hard time recruiting and retaining talent

Key Digital Marketing Roles

<u>Website Architect</u> defines the scope of website content with respect to copy, visuals, and interaction with prospects and customers (not a graphic designer, copywriter, or computer programmer, but someone who can understand the needs and feasibilities and can write briefs for all three previously mentioned parties).

There is a perfect analogy here with a traditional architect who matches aesthetic, financial, and functional specifications for a beautiful new building with what is technically feasible in construction technologies today. An architect provides a blueprint to be implemented by a general contractor and subcontractors.

The cost of architects in traditional construction is about 20% of the total cost of the building and nobody questions the importance of their contributions. On the other hand, we see a lot of websites built by inexperienced, low-paid graphic designers or computer programmers who cannot be expected to span all of these skill sets. The results are a plethora of poorly designed sites with irrelevant content and confusing navigation.

<u>Copywriter</u> role is growing as websites get penalized by Google for poor and/or irrelevant content (even poor grammar, repetitions, and misspellings).

On a positive note, creating unique and engaging content is very important in grabbing the reader's attention, which drives web traffic. This demand is reflected in hourly rates for good copywriters that exceed the rates paid to programmers. If you are a student thinking about working in marketing, make sure to take as many writing classes as you can. You can even freelance writing web content while going to school.

Email marketing expert knows that email does not get a lot of credit but it is one of the most effective digital marketing channels. It requires good command of the local language, but not a lot of technical skills as today's email marketing programs are very easy to use and analyze.

Data analyst brings expertise in web traffic, email effectiveness, social media sentiments, advertising conversion rates, sales, and profitability, supplemented with the ability to visualize and communicate results to senior management. The last step involves good writing skills as well, so investment in writing education is a great idea anyway.

- Website architect
- Copywriter
- Email marketer
- Data analyst

These four highly desirable skills have another advantage in today's global marketplace. They cannot be easily outsourced to overseas production centers. Writing requires excellent native spoken and written language skills. The architect also needs to be a fluent communicator orally and in writing with an excellent knowledge of the business. And the data analyst certainly cannot be effective without an intimate knowledge of the business and proximity to executives to understand the local 4 Ps—problems, priorities, personalities, and politics.

The following skills can be sourced from anywhere in the world as long as professionals involved have a basic knowledge of the local language. With strong briefs written by a good architect, these skills can be managed remotely.

- Graphic designer
- Video production
- Technical web programmer
- Database programmer

GREG GUTKOWSKI

For more in depth discussion on digital marketing, you may want to get my bestselling book *9 Best Kept Secrets of B2B Digital Marketing* available on Amazon.

4
PUBLIC RELATIONS
AND REPUTATION MANAGEMENT

'Character is like a tree and reputation like a shadow. The shadow is what we think of it; the tree is the real thing.' Abraham Lincoln

Today, the practice of public relations is all about skillful management of social media and email campaigns. The classical PR model that attempts to influence journalists to pick up their version of the truth can only be effective with the heavy use of social media channels including Facebook, Twitter, LinkedIn, Instagram, Pinterest, and now even Snapchat.

The name of the game is to spread the message as wide and as frequently as possible. Social media are the perfect channel for that. Publishing on social media is less expensive when compared to traditional print publications.

Social media posts provide links to the main websites where visitors can sign up for more updates or newsletters to be delivered in the future by email.

Public relations can take advantage of precise targeting, especially on Facebook and LinkedIn. This involves relatively inexpensive advertising. So, PR organizations had to learn how to do digital advertising and the subsequent data analysis.

Analyzing social media reach and sentiments and measuring how they change over time provide yet more powerful tools for PR campaigns. Social media analytics require specific skills that PR agencies did not have or need before.

When BP was faced with the Gulf of Mexico oil spill crisis in 2010, their PR professionals purchased a lot of ads on Google tied to searches such as 'oil spill', 'BP oil spill', 'Deepwater Horizon spill', and 'Gulf of Mexico spill'. Clicking on a subsequent Google ad led to BP's website containing the PR content, including the description of the clean-up effort, statements by executives, contact information, etc.

Thus, BP's public relations efforts got directly tied to Google advertising. By the way, BP also made a big effort to show up organically in Google by investing in search engine optimization (SEO) upgrades that resulted in BP's ad and web pages displaying when users entered the aforementioned keywords or phrases.

Type 'BP spill' in Google and BP is there in search results—in the first position with their Google ad and the second position organically, just after the Wikipedia article describing this accident. When you click on their listings you are brought to a BP page devoted to the restoration of the spill.

These pages have links to BP social media, which insure that a consistent message is spread around. Thus, the circle between advertising, website presence, and social media has been made.

PR agencies today remind me more of a digital marketing agency as they need almost identical skills to spread their message. The lines between PR, digital marketing, and advertising are blurring all the time.

- Social media dependence
- Precise targeting on Facebook and LinkedIn
- Sentiment analysis
- BP oil spill

Reputation Management

Reputation management is a subset of PR and involves the management of testimonials, evaluations, and opinions made on social media or websites and directly related to the quality of products and services offered by the organization. The impact of having poor reviews can be huge, especially if it is not quickly and immediately addressed. On the other hand, the value of good reviews cannot be overestimated.

A best practice of reputation management for business is to address any complaints directly and publically online as quickly as possible by asking for a live conversation to understand and possibly remedy the situation. For that, you need to be able to monitor all negative comments that may show up on your social media accounts as well as public posts on Twitter or Yelp and be alerted in real time. There are tools on the market to set up such alerts.

Another good practice is to proactively solicit good reviews from satisfied customers and post them on your website and social media accounts. This is a very good strategy to counter any negative reviews, which can never be avoided but can be minimized and marginalized.

Reputation management can also involve managing your personal information on social media, especially if your past posts no longer project the desired image. This is a very widespread problem with the younger audience who, in the past, may have posted very juvenile content that is now visible to potential hiring managers.

On a personal front, one strategy is to remove links to the undesirable content (which could be time consuming and/or impossible). Another strategy is to counter the negatives with a highly professional profile on LinkedIn and Facebook as well as the personal website, demonstrating a consistent message.

The digital skills associated with reputation management do not vary from skills required to be effective in a digital marketing agency.

- Subset of PR
- Management of online testimonials, evaluations and opinions
- Immediate reaction
- Active solicitation
- Personal reputation management

5
SALES

'So long as new ideas are created, sales will continue to reach new highs.'
Dorothea Brande

In sales, information is power. This is especially true the larger the sale and the more decision makers and influencers are involved.

Sales and ordering processes can be streamlined by using Customer Relationships Management (CRM) systems such as salesforce.com or Pipedrive. Sales intelligence can be greatly enhanced by monitoring the social media activities of prospects and competitors as well as real time tracking of web visitors.

Long sales cycles

Imagine a 12-month cycle to sell a multimillion-dollar contract to a Fortune 1000 company. On your end, beside yourself as a sales executive, there could be several more people in your organization who are involved: a product specialist from corporate, local pre-sales consultant, your manager, and your office administrative support staff.

On the other side of the transaction, there is a selection committee made up of 10 members who meet once per month. The members range from a VP to their admin person. In the process, you have to answer 40 questions on the RFP (request for proposal). You will be communicating via email and phone with most of the members.

How are you going to manage this process, track all this information over 12 months, and continually report progress to your anxious manager waiting for your big possible win to hit the books so the whole branch can get the annual bonus?

- 12+ month sales cycle
- Multiple players
  - Own support
  - Selection committee
- Request for proposal (RFP)
- From VP to admin person
- Constant communication and coordination

CRM to the rescue

The only way to do it effectively is to have a system that records all these interactions in one place, each with a time stamp.

There are several systems on the market to support such complex undertakings. They are called CRM for Customer Relationship Management.

Every phone call and every email regarding this sale is automatically logged. Dialing a phone number automatically logs the call timing and duration. A sales rep fills out other information, such as specifics on the next steps.

- One place
- Time stamp on all interactions
- Customer Relationship Management systems
- Every interaction logged either manually or automatically
  - Call
  - Email/document sent
  - Visit
  - Conversation

Digital 'snooping'

The sales cycle starts with the careful analysis of the social media profiles and posts of all 10 selection committee members. The sales rep needs access to LinkedIn, Twitter, Facebook, and possibly Pinterest and Instagram.

The analysis will reveal the members' professional and personal backgrounds, schools they went to, as well as their hobbies, interests, the publications they read, etc. LinkedIn would reveal that our rep's best buddy went to school with the VP. A separate entry will be made in the CRM for each of the committee members. Each one will have automatic look-up of their social media profile. A good sales rep will look for any common touch points to build rapport.

Next is a competitive analysis. What do we know about the competition, their products? Social media, as well as analysis of the competition's websites, will provide a lot of useful information.

Maybe there are a lot of complaints on Twitter about the competitive products. Maybe a competitor is experiencing serious financial problems. You need to examine recent articles (via subscription to sites such as Feedly or Scoop.it) and set up Google alerts.

A separate entry will be created in CRM for each competitor. Again, such information may mean the difference between winning or losing a multimillion-dollar sale.

- Social media
  - ○ Profiles (personal and corporate)
  - ○ Tweets, posts, discussions
- Websites
- Articles
- Google alerts

RFP Responses

Following that, there will be your response to the RFP. On your side, you will need input from corporate, your manager, and the cooperation of an admin to put it all together and FedEx it to the client. How are you going to track all these interactions and their timing?

Again, CRM and document management systems come to the rescue. All revisions and communication steps will be logged with exact time stamps.

- Response to RFP
- Document management / version management
- Responding to additional questions

Patience

Then, a rep will be alerted automatically by CRM that there were a lot of searches on the corporate website from the prospective customer site (this can be tracked by IP address). A more detailed analysis shows that the most and the longest visits were on pages devoted to product specs and testimonials. So far so good.

Next, for some unexplained reason, things go silent for 2 months. None of the members responded to phone calls or opened an email from our sales rep (email systems allow for tracking of opened emails). This is not a good sign. Something serious must be going on at the prospective customer. Our rep finds relevant articles on the prospect's business and emails them to maintain visibility without looking desperate.

Finally, a single simple tweet from the CEO of the prospective company announces a major acquisition.

So it's reasonable to expect that our sale got delayed due to that event and our sales cycle is still alive.

During these ups and downs, the sales manager and his boss are very interested in the status. No problem; they can log in to the CRM and get an update anytime they want.

Finally, our rep gets invited back for the negotiations. They take about 3 tense weeks and everyone wants a daily status update.
After 3 weeks, the agreement is signed. At year-end, a nice bonus arrives for everyone involved.

- Visits to your website
- Prospect goes silent
- Managing your management's expectations
- Monitoring prospect's activities
- Contract finally signed!

The end of a story - or is it?

A new phase has just been born and it's called....customer service.

Using the same CRM, all interactions with the new customer are logged in, this time by customer service reps. Any implementation hiccups, complaints, or delays are very well known to our rep who is still in charge of managing the overall relationship.

New members of the customer's organization are added to CRM. Our sales rep watches every step of implementation and checks with his primary contact to see if the new customer is satisfied. Everything is going relatively smoothly and the new customer brags on social media that they got a great deal. The contract gets renewed for another year.

Our rep learns that the new customer contemplates rolling out the new product to all subsidiaries. A very enticing proposal with a nice discount is proposed. In March of the following year, the customer puts in an order five times as big as the original one.

- After the sale need to manage implementation
- Switching to customer service mode
- Managing hiccups, complaints and delays
- Upselling
- Hard to manage such complexity without many digital tools

Summary

CRM facilitated successful management of multi-step, multi-person, multi-organization, multi-state sales process that involved competitive research, analysis of social media and web traffic, multiple email interactions, in-person visits, call tracking, internal reporting and communication, and RFP generation—all from a single platform.

It made the whole team more productive, better informed, and satisfied. It flagged the opportunity for a big upsell and made the customer very happy (not to mention the sales rep's manager—and the rep, too).

In the past, it was rather hard to manage such a process using separate Outlook emails, Excel spreadsheets, Word documents, tons of paper, and constant interruptions from nervous managers seeking updates.

A lot of balls were dropped and a lot of things fell through the cracks.

The integration of CRMs with social media, web visit analysis, document management, email campaigns, and their tracking has a profound positive impact on complex sales processes.

GREG GUTKOWSKI

The functionalities we have just described are almost identical to digital marketing activities. And indeed, many CRM vendors are adding features to their systems that blend digital marketing functions such as web analytics, email, and social media management with existing tracking and document management capabilities.

6
FINANCE, COMPLIANCE, AND AUDIT

'Beware of little expenses. A small leak will sink a great ship.'
Benjamin Franklin

Finance and accounting are probably the most digitized processes, just after IT. Accounting was the first and the easiest business process to be digitized as it involved relatively small volumes of data made up mostly of numbers.

The data tends to be very clean, as ledgers have to balance to zero variance. In addition, financial professionals tend to be very analytical and easy to train on financial and accounting systems. All these facts contributed to the early adoption of digital financial processes.

Finance

Nevertheless, finance can greatly benefit from much more detailed and frequent measurements of various processes. This may allow for better allocation of direct costs, thus leading to better pricing and enhanced profitability analysis.

This is especially true with respect to marketing and manufacturing processes where today, a lot of costs are allocated as overhead, thus precluding more granular discovery of profit drivers.

In layman's terms, it means that Finance does not know the actual cost of producing a unit of product X. This in turn means that pricing for this product may not cover the cost of making it, or it's too high and becomes non-competitive. As competition intensifies, one could greatly benefit from a precise knowledge of the real cost of production.

For example, in many manufacturing processes, the actual usage of compressed air and electricity per a particular run of production is unknown. This is because there are no meters tracking the power usage of the motors running air compressors and the actual production line. In some manufacturing processes, compressed air is a significant percentage of production cost. Today, compressed air and the power usage may be allocated based on an arbitrary formula not reflecting the actual amounts used.

You can only solve this problem by measuring power consumption in real time by all electrical motors, including motors powering air compressors.

In summary, the more detailed the measurement, the more precise the picture of profitability. This is of growing importance in the super competitive global economy.

- The most digitized off all business processes
- Clean and small databases of mostly numbers
- Can benefit from more detailed measurement
- Better allocation of direct costs
  - Profit analysis
  - Pricing
- Important in highly competitive global economy

Compliance/Audits

Any process that is digitally tracked with the right precision can provide a valuable audit. This becomes very handy in case of malfunction, or to prove regulatory compliance.

Let's say we have noticed that there are a lot of warranty returns on product A. Product A is made up of 45 components. A historical analysis of all production steps and inputs shows that only component number 27 is from a different part provider in the malfunctioning product.

The subsequent analysis of all production steps showed that component number 27 was stored in an unheated Minnesota warehouse for 4 months of winter there. Conclusion: there was nothing wrong with component #27 other than inappropriate storage. We do not need to recall component #27, we need to keep in it a heated warehouse.

The lack of tracking the detailed steps in production precluded the analysis of E Coli contamination of produce several years ago. Customers who bought lettuce were getting sick, but the grocery store could not track a poisonous batch of lettuce as there were no separate labels affixed to them.

The grocery store did not track each farmer individually and thus could not isolate which farm the contamination came from. This is probably the best example to support the old adage that you cannot manage if you cannot measure.

Today, this situation could be easily solved by placing an RFID chip on each crate to identify the farm the lettuce came from.

A more advanced example involves the tracking of failures of all the parts on a jet plane to understand the root cause of larger system failures, such as wings or landing gear.

An example of similar complexity is the detailed tracking of all medical steps, procedures, drugs, and treatments used in patient care. It can be used in defending lawsuits or, on a more positive note, in understanding if all the right steps were taken at the right time and sequence.

An additional benefit could be that the data collected on all treatments of the same disease may lead to the discovery of the best path to patient recovery.

- Analysis of malfunctions or failures
- To improve quality
- To prove compliance
- To defend lawsuits

7
INFORMATION TECHNOLOGIES

'Everybody gets so much information all day long that they lose their common sense.'
Gertrude Stein

Last but not least are IT departments responsible for managing all digital technologies from desktop computers and smartphones, to databases, data networks, and security. Like accounting, they may be 100% digital, but they may have functionally disconnected parts.

IT is the *de facto* electronic guardian of all the processes described earlier, but each process may be supported by a different system. These systems usually are of different vintage, written in different computer languages, and therefore seldom sharing the underlying data. The data resides in separate silos.

For example, marketing data is separate from sales data and from actual cost data. Therefore, it is impossible to perform a simple analysis of what the marketing program cost, how it contributed to what product sales, and what was the overall profitability by product after taking warranty returns into account.

- The most digitized off all processes
- Digital does not always translate to interoperable
- Data in separate silos

IT Paradox

Paradoxically, IT departments may be very seriously disrupted by the digital revolution. Fast telecommunication networks and very inexpensive data storage led to the new business model whereby the majority of technical IT functions can be outsourced to third party providers. This includes procurement and maintenance of hardware, operating systems, security, user authentications—the' digital plumbing' of any business.

The fancy marketing term for this outsourcing is referred to as 'cloud' computing. In reality, it is an example of the division of labor concept where 'digital plumbing' management can be left to more efficient 'digital plumbers' who specialize in managing thousands of computer servers under one roof for a fraction of the cost it takes the average IT department.

This concept is similar to 'outsourcing' our electricity production to a local power plant instead of all of us running our own diesel powered generators. Less noise, less pollution, and the cost per kilowatt hour is much less. Also, you only pay for the electricity you use every month instead of having to buy an expensive generator up front. The power plant also worries about meeting higher demand during the peaks of hot and cold seasons.

Gartner, a leading market research firm, forecasts that 50% of all internal IT and business services will migrate to the cloud by 2020. This does not bode well for technical professionals whose job today is to manage and maintain hardware, networks, and security for their current employers.

By the way, cloud computing is not going to impact the demand for creative software developers and data analysts—they will just be accessing computers somewhere in the cloud.

I think that Gartner is right, and this trend will impact smaller companies much more than larger enterprises. Smaller businesses are the ones who do not want and do not know how to manage 'digital plumbing' and can least afford full time computer technicians on staff. They are just interested in how to leverage existing technology to improve their operations and profits.

- Paradox of shrinking IT departments in the age of digital
- Cloud computing - digital plumbing
- Compelling reason to outsource 'digital plumbing' to a cloud

8
SECURITY AND PRIVACY
Digital Achilles Heel

So far we have painted a very optimistic picture of the digital revolution having a profound impact on economic growth.

However, in addition to the data integrity issues we discussed earlier, there are other two large looming issues of even higher severity and importance. They are data security and privacy.

Security and privacy are completely intertwined as there is no privacy without security. However, privacy can be violated even with the best security when the right privacy policies are not in place.

Security

Security is of the utmost importance. Only with good security solutions will the adoption of all these great digital concepts move forward to benefit our society. Otherwise, business managers will hesitate to take on so much risk.

Security is both a technical and organizational challenge. We need to balance convenience with safety. Too much security will slow down transactions and thus economic development. Too little security will have a similarly chilling effect on the economy as people will not engage as much as they would if they felt safe.

People are the weakest link in security. Disgruntled, careless, or untrained employees account for most security breaches.

Therefore, the risk of security breaches will always be there. It can be managed and mitigated, but it cannot be eliminated. This is a continuous problem—it cannot be 'fixed' at one time.

As long as humans are involved, there will be security challenges. After all, the history of humankind is also a history of inventing the best locks and the corresponding lock picks.

- Utmost importance
- Security vs. convenience
- People are the biggest vulnerability
- Mitigate risk - risk will always be there
- Continuous problem - cannot be just 'fixed' one time

Privacy - Digital right to be left alone

Privacy issues will have to be dealt with via legislation. We already have a precedent in the U.S. with respect to the privacy of our medical records. These privacy provisions are captured and enforced by HIPAA regulations (The Health Insurance Portability and Accountability Act of 1996).

We see no technical reason why the same protection cannot be extended to our personal data that we ourselves generate while interacting on the Internet. Every one of us should have a right to opt in or out of our own personal data sharing with various Internet providers and expect that these providers will honor the agreement under the penalty of law.

After all, the content of our regular mail is not accessible to the U.S. Post Office for sale. By putting our paper letters in a sealed envelope and affixing a postage stamp, we enter into an explicit contract with the Post Office that the privacy of our content is protected and won't be snooped on. If anybody gets caught opening and reading our old fashioned paper letters, they will end up in a state penitentiary as opposed to enriching themselves selling our private information.

"In a May 2014 ruling by the Court of Justice of the European Union, the court decided that users have the right to ask search engines like Google to remove results for queries that include their name. To qualify, the results shown would need to be inadequate, irrelevant, no longer relevant, or excessive." This ruling, however, does not apply to public figures.

I think that this is a move in the right direction. We should have full rights to opt in and opt out of sharing our personal information, and that right should be strictly enforced.

We have rights to our private property and we can trade them on the market. There is no reason we cannot do the same with the information we authored ourselves. As HIPAA shows, this is doable.

It may involve some costs, but the social media giants have plenty of cash to pay for such protection. They made this money by selling our personal information to advertisers, so it should be their responsibility to guard it and to be severely punished when they breach that trust. After all, hacking is a crime today.

In another development, The United States House of Representatives is currently working on the Intimate Privacy Protection Act, a bipartisan bill that would make it illegal to distribute explicit private images without the consent of the people involved.

It would stipulate criminal punishment for third parties who profit from the sale of such material. The bill was prompted by Gawker's publishing private erotic videos of Hulk Hogan.

This is another step in the right direction. The law is slowly catching up with the digital revolution.

Store your data in the bank

There is an interesting idea afloat of using banks to store and guard the private data we generate. Just like money, our privacy is valuable and the lack of it may wreak havoc on our lives.

Whether it is a bank or another 3rd party, I admit I like the idea in general. It makes a lot of sense. Let the top professionals help us store and guard our most precious assets that are sometimes more valuable than money itself.

Technically, it is already feasible. Just like your medical records, everyone can have a file with all the things that they have ever generated digitally. Then an easy interface would allow us to indicate what information is to be exchanged with whom based on a set of rules.

The exchange of information will take place over standard APIs.

For this process to work, a bullet-proof audit trail needs to be a part of it. Without it, there would be no trust and no way to enforce the rules.

Blockchain technologies would be perfect for such an application, as they provide a reliable and sustainable audit trail. I can imagine paying $5 to $10 per month to have my information stored and guarded by top security professionals, assuring selective access based on my stated preferences.

I think we will see a lot of positive activities around privacy issues very soon, as a larger portion of the electorate is becoming aware of all the ramifications of security breaches and data exposure. This in turn, puts the necessary pressure on legislators to address this serious issue. I suspect we will have this problem solved in the next 10 years, just like we solved the problem with the privacy of our snail mail.

- Legislation and enforcement is the only answer
- HIPAA precedence
- Protection for personal data as for medical records
- Right to be removed
- Intimate Privacy Protection Act
- Privacy protections by the 3rd parties

9
SUMMARY

Paradoxically for many companies, the problem is not the lack of software and/or technology.

The problem is absorbing what is already out there.

Case in point: To run a company and/or improve business performance, we use 6-10 different software systems:

1. Social media feeds - all the 'likes', retweets, comments, etc.
2. Online advertising - AdWords and/or Facebook Ads
3. Web analytics
4. Email
5. CRM or sales management
6. Fulfillment/Point of sale
7. Human resources/recruiting
8. Project management and/or production
9. Phone system
10. Finance/Accounting

All companies, ranging from Fortune 500s to mom-and-pop shops, perform most of these tasks. Not always with dedicated systems—Excel often comes to the rescue.

Regardless of the degree of specialization and automation, all of these systems require a lot of learning, training, and support. This is not just about the mechanics of using software. It's also about the *right way* to do things.

Automating ineffective tasks is pointless. However, even when doing the right things, it takes time to acquire skills on the mechanics of using a new system. It takes a lot of learning to run an AdWords campaign, analyze website traffic, set up drip email campaigns, configure and teach CRM, or train and implement a new ordering system. It takes months or even years to get the staff up to speed to take advantage of the software that has already been acquired.

Human ability to absorb technological change is not going to expand anytime soon. Actually, I believe that most of us are at capacity already.

Nevertheless, most software tools offer very similar business functionalities despite the marketing spin of competing vendors. Thus, the major productivity bottleneck is not the selection or acquisition of the right software. The major bottleneck is what to do with the new system and how to make the staff proficient at using it.

This is analogous to the challenges of transportation. There are a lot of almost identical trucks, containers, cargo carriers, and warehouses. However, the winners are those who know how to manage the supply chain and arm their staff with the relevant skills and knowledge to align all the moving parts for profit.

The logical conclusion to this argument is that *skills and knowledge* are the major bottlenecks to the utilization of technology and not the lack of technology itself.

Many companies have already bitten off more software than we can digitally chew. The result is digital indigestion, manifesting itself in using the wrong software for the wrong task, not using the features we already paid for, and not understanding how technology impacts performance.

The only remedy for such a misalignment is **more education on what to do, how to do it, and how to analyze if it works** in the context of existing business software.

PART IV
DIGITAL CONCEPTS

1
INTRODUCTION
Complex Made Simple

In this section, we will go over basic digital terminology. Terminology associated with the digital revolution can be quite confusing. There are several reasons for that.

One reason is that technology vendors come up with marketing terms in an attempt to brand their new products and services. Given their large promotional budgets, they coin certain creative terms such as 'cloud computing'. The term becomes a popular marketing name, but means different things to different people and confuses them.

The other reason is an attempt to describe old concepts using new terms to underscore the growing importance of existing phenomena. Twenty years, ago we had EIS (Executive Information Systems), then DSS (Decision Support Systems), followed by OLAP (Online Analytical Processing), Data Mining, and finally today BI (Business Intelligence) systems. However, over all these years, they've all been doing exactly the same thing; i.e., analyzing data and creating managerial charts and reports.

Data scientist vs. old fashioned 'statistician' or 'data analyst' is another good example. Data scientist just sounds more 'cool' but the job responsibilities of analyzing data have been the same for the last century...

Yet, another example is Big Data, denoting just…. more data.

- Branding of new products and services
- Growing importance of old concepts

- EIS, DSS, OLAP, Data Mining, BI = analyze and present data
- Data scientist = Data Analyst
- Big Data = lots of data

Let's me explain all of these concepts in plain English stripped of marketing spin. We will decipher the following terms/technologies:

- Cloud Computing
- Internet of Things
- SMAC
- Artificial Intelligence
- Machine Learning
- Big Data
- Analytics
- Predictive Analytics
- Business Intelligence
- Data Mining, Data Warehouse, Data Mart, Data Lake
- 3D Printing
- Robotics
- Augmented Reality
- Virtual Reality

The more things change, the more they remain the same

Please, keep in mind that little has changed in the field of computer science since the 1970s.

There were computers then, and we've had them exchanging data remotely since 1969. We were able to send live pictures and audio from the Moon and back and display it on our TVs. Satellites have been with us since 1958. Phones and color TV screens as well. So, from the concept perspective, not much new has happened.

What *is* new is the increase in the power of computing with a simultaneous drop in cost at a rate that surprised even the most optimistic prognosticators of the time.

Today, a new Android phone can be had for about $100 and has more computing and telecommunication power than took us to the moon and back.

The result is that we can do things very fast, very easily, and very cheaply that used to be very slow, very hard, and extremely expensive. That is all from the academic perspective.

However, from the practical perspective, this allows us to create and use many new products and services that were virtually impossible to imagine just a few years ago. Just as it was hard for our great-grandparents to envision electricity at home and for our grandparents to imagine cars, planes, and color TV.

The technologies we will be discussing are just tools. They have no value if not plugged into processes involving people–mostly customers—and their support.

None of the digital technologies invented by humans can stand alone on its own merit. They are tremendously valuable only as a part of a process involving people. There is no better quote that captures this sentiment than,

> *'Computers are incredibly fast, accurate, and stupid:*
> *humans are incredibly slow, inaccurate and brilliant;*
> *together they are powerful beyond imagination.'*
> *Unknown*

2
CLOUD COMPUTING

'Cloud computing is a great euphemism for centralization
of computer services under one server.'
Evgeny Morozov

Conceptually, cloud computing services are similar to electricity production. Instead of every household having to pay for its own power generator up front, install it, and maintain it, we have a network of electrical wires connected to the local power plant. Then, we pay as we go only for the electricity we use.

The same analogy holds for municipal water and sewage services. Instead of everyone having an underground water pump and a septic field, we have a central intake of fresh water and sewage treatment plants.

- Similar concept to electrical grid
- Municipal water

Business software

Cloud services are based on a very compelling value proposition. Instead of installing and maintaining software and hardware at your office, you subscribe to a service hosted on remote servers and accessible via the Internet at a fraction of the cost. This 'digital plumbing' includes procurement and maintenance of hardware and software servers, networks, access control, security, data storage, backups, and a redundant environment for testing and development.

- 'Digital plumbing'
- Procurement and maintenance of hardware and software
- Computer networks
- Access control & security
- Data storage & backup
- Redundancy for testing

Software in the cloud

In the cloud, you would put all the software needed to run your business. In your offices, which could be far away, all you need is an Internet browser, a fast Internet connection, and a password.

Thus, you can just concentrate on leveraging the digital technologies in your existing processes and/or create new systems to enhance, for example, the customer experience instead of worrying about security, upgrading hardware and software, and maintaining communication networks.

- Compelling value proposition
- All you need is browser, fast Internet connection and a password
- Concentrate on adding value to business
- Don't worry about the 'digital plumbing'
- Leave it to the pros

Cost of Storage vs. Amounts of Data

The data storage cost went down almost 4 times over just 5 years. This is inversely correlated to the amount of total data on the Internet. Today, the cost of storing data is almost zero. It costs more to manage it than to store it.

The dramatically decreasing prices of software, hardware, and telecommunications is what made cloud services possible.

Cloud computing is a clever marketing term, but in the technical sense, it is nothing more than distributed computing enabled by Internet connectivity. Cloud hosting companies specialize in providing all the 'digital plumbing'. Due to economies of scale, cloud vendors can provide the 'digital plumbing' services at a fraction of the cost.

This model is especially attractive to smaller companies who do not have, or cannot afford, a dedicated IT professional to install and maintain hardware and software.

- Clever marketing term
- Distributed computing enabled by fast connectivity
- Specialization
- Economies of scale
- Very attractive, especially to smaller companies

The power of software and hardware democratized

Cloud-based services brought about professional grade digital technology solutions at very low price points. In the past, only large companies could afford to buy and install expensive hardware and software at their premises, as telecommunication prices were prohibitive to smaller players.

Software companies charged millions per installation because their costs were spread among very few customers. This expensive software and hardware provided a competitive advantage, as smaller players could not afford it.

Not anymore. The power of software and hardware has become democratized. Cloud software and business software vendors can now charge much less per user, as they can access a much larger user base worldwide.

Anyone can afford a world class CRM (Customer Relationship Management) system for $20 per user per month. What used to cost millions is now very inexpensive.

- Great products at low prices
- Democratization of software and hardware power
- Everyone can afford the 'latest and greatest'

Advantages of cloud computing

Here are the 4 major advantages of cloud services:

- Concentrate on leveraging digital technologies to generate revenues and/or cutting costs rather than managing 'digital plumbing'
- Trade capital purchase for monthly service expense

- Pay as you go. If you need more computing power around the peak shopping season, you do not need to buy more computers and then have them sit idle for the rest of the year. Just pay for temporary access to more computing power. Your total cost of IT will be lower when leveraging cloud services
- Have top professionals guard your digital assets. Today, any company needs at least 3 full time computer security professionals to effectively guard their business. Most smaller enterprises cannot afford such expense and as a result a lot of them are highly vulnerable to hacking.

Good news - bad news

Cloud computing is not good news for computer technicians that currently manage the 'digital plumbing' for their employers. Nevertheless, it is a very good trend, especially for any new business starting from scratch, as they can concentrate on growing their business by leveraging the latest inexpensive software and avoiding non-productive technical challenges associated with 'digital plumbing'.

- Eliminates IT infrastructure jobs
- Lowers the 'digital plumbing' cost
- Increases effectiveness and efficiency of business operations

3
INTERNET OF THINGS
AND SMAC

'The Internet is not just one thing, it's a collection of things - of numerous communications networks that all speak the same digital language.'
Jim Clark

Think about the Internet of Things (IoT) as a digitally connected world that includes houses and their appliances, cameras, buildings, factories and their equipment, cars, trucks, ships, drones, and airplanes—all being able to 'talk to each other'.

Here is Wikipedia's definition of IoT: "The network of physical devices, vehicles, buildings, and other items—embedded with electronics, software, sensors, and network connectivity that enable these objects to collect and exchange data."

I would add… This collection and exchange of data allows for remote sensing, controlling, alerting, communicating, and managing physical objects.

According to a Gartner Inc. forecast, there will be 6.4 billion connected things in use worldwide in 2016 . And it's expected to grow to 21 billion by 2020.

- The network of physical devices
- Remote:
  - Sensing
  - Alerting
  - Controlling

- o Communicating
- o Managing
- Over 6 billion connected devices In 2016
- 21 billion connected devices by 2020

Smartphone is IOT

A smartphone is a perfect example of an IoT node. It combines all these functionalities and more. Indeed, a smartphone is already a major hub for a lot of IoT applications including geo location, tracking fitness and vital signs via Bluetooth, trip directions, speech and image recognition, remote control of home security and appliances, and chasing Pokemon, to name a few.

- Smartphone as a perfect IoT node
    - o Receives and sends data
    - o Senses location, vibration, altitude
    - o Speech and image recognition
    - o Video and voice recording and playback

IOT applications

A good example of an IoT application is the Navistar service alerting car owners that tire pressure on their car is getting too low but is not alarming yet (in case of serious problems, drivers get notifications on their dashboard).

The cost of sensors to measure tire pressure as well as the cost of data transmission went down so much that it became economical to install sensors on each wheel, transmit the data via a satellite, and put it in an email to the customer. The same service would remotely open my car door if somebody locks themselves out (after the operator verifies their identity).

Other IoT examples include humidity and pH sensors placed in the soil and transmitting that information to irrigation and fertilization systems. The amount of water and fertilizer applied varies depending on the readings from these sensors. The savings can amount to over 20% of water, electricity, and fertilizer.

A very innovative and very inexpensive IoT application is one that warns of avalanches or mudslides. All you need is two rods with sensors allowing for measurement of their relative distance from each other. You stick one rod uphill in the solid ground and put the other downhill in the snow or mud. When the distance starts to exceed the predefined threshold level, the application transmits that information as an alert about the immediate danger of an avalanche or a mudslide.

How much would you pay for such an application if you were the owner of a ski resort?

The ultimate easy-to-use IoT application, though very sophisticated behind the scenes, is a self-driving car. It is based on numerous real time sensors working with each other to steer the vehicle in the desired direction while avoiding foreign objects.

- Remote car diagnostics
- Optimal irrigation and fertilization
- Avalanche, mudslide alerts
- Self driving cars, tractors, ships

IOT summary

IoT works very well when the benefit of monitoring and optimization exceeds the cost of sensors and data transmission. With the ongoing decrease in cost of sensors and digital technologies, there will be more IoT applications. Some of them may even be hard to imagine now.

In summary, the Internet of Things is a big part of the digital revolution. It has a unique name to denote physical nodes sensing and exchanging information. However, from the process and analysis perspective, it is just another complex business process with a lot of data.

- Future applications may be hard to imagine now
- Cost of sensors and data communication and analysis is going down
- Marketing concept - not technical or analytical
- Just another complex business problem with lots of data

SMAC - Social, Mobile, Analytics, Cloud

Several years ago, Gartner introduced a framework called SMAC for the convergence of social, mobile, analytics, and cloud technologies. The idea is that these 4 components will be an integral part of any business application going forward. Thus, IT departments should have architectural plans reflecting that fusion.

- PGA Tour is perfect example
- The latest phase in computing platforms
- Marketing concept - not technical or analytical
- Just another complex business process with lots of data

We presented a great example of SMAC while discussing the digital revolution at the PGA Tour and other sporting events. Data on the golf game is being collected via cameras, microphones, and radar, analyzed in real time, and then shared socially on mobile devices among players, coaches, and spectators.

Gartner treats SMAC as a the latest phase in the evolution of computing platforms that started with the mainframe computer, then the PC (Personal Computer), then the Internet (Web), and now SMAC. It is a term very popular among top IT management.

One may wonder what is the difference between IoT and SMAC? In our judgment, not that much, nor is the difference important—both reflect the digital technology universe and digital processes.

IoT and SMAC, like Artificial Intelligence and Machine Learning, are marketing concepts that are overlapping and could be little confusing.

4
ARTIFICIAL INTELLIGENCE
AND MACHINE LEARNING

Speaking of Artificial Intelligence (AI) and Machine Learning (ML)... We consider them to be just marketing terms. From the computer science and academic perspective, these are just very sophisticated software algorithms used against a variety of either very complex and/or voluminous data.

These algorithms require a lot of computing power or a lot of algorithmic logic, or both, to accomplish the task of optimizing a process. Algorithms are written by humans based on their business problem knowledge combined with their experience in computer science, and mathematics, statistics, psychology, linguistics, and neuroscience.

Is speech recognition an example of artificial intelligence? We think not. It is just an optimal way to recognize speech.

- Require powerful algorithms
- May require a lot of computing power
- Written by humans
- Just another optimization process
- Intelligence is in writing and implementing algorithms

Several years ago, optical character recognition (OCR), or turning scanned text to data, was considered AI, until it became a boring but very productive routine.

At the end of the day, at the processing level, all data is just a bunch of 0s and 1s, whether it's photos, video, audio, text, or numbers or a combination of these.

There is no artificial intelligence or machine learning. The intelligence and learning are in the development and implementation of algorithms that can take advantage of the available data and existing computer power.

AI is just a tech marketing term used to sell more software, hardware, services, and research around mathematical algorithms that have been around for years. The only new things are the increased computing power and more data that we can feed it. More power seldom makes things more intelligent.

More data may help, but that data needs to be relevant, timely, correct, and granular enough to make the whole concept work. The problem is that we lack the right data to explain most of the problems we are trying to solve today (despite collecting tons of data in general).

Corvette with not tires

In meteorology, we cannot even predict the weather in our towns in the next 12 hours so we can leave our umbrellas behind. Why not? Because we do not have enough granular atmospheric data for our weather prediction models. Collecting relevant weather data is prohibitively expensive so our weather stations are sparsely located.

In medical research, we do not have enough granular, longitudinal, reliable, consistent, and clean data to learn what causes our bodies to stop producing insulin, or what causes most cancers or even a common flu. We don't even have a consistent medical patient records database to manage basic healthcare needs!

In business, 99% of companies have data in silos of marketing, sales, customer service, and finance not 'talking' to each other, which prevents us from the basic discovery of what really drives profits. Thus, a lot of resources are wasted on guesstimates. Case in point: it is almost impossible to attribute actual sales to most social media posts (not ads). The same is true with most radio, TV, and print advertising.

In economics, despite tons of data collected by the government and Wall Street, one can hardly spot down-cycles and warn the public about them. Remember the dot.com and 2008 crashes?

In politics, during the last U.S. elections, the media told us that one candidate had a more than 95% chance of winning just a few days before we learned otherwise. It was not the lack of computing power that led to such a conclusion.

We do well with algorithms when the data is clean, relevant, and plentiful. For example, computers can identify a malignant tumor from a high-resolution scan, but only because there are enough relevant pixels in the picture (computers are fed thousands of pictures with affected and healthy patient data so they can 'learn' from comparing the two sets). Yet, the same computer does not know what caused this tumor or how to cure it….as it lacks appropriate data in the first place.

In summary, we do not have the relevant data (granular, timely, and correct) to solve the majority of problems faced by humanity today, including healthcare, economy, weather, marketing, and politics.

Thus, the Achilles heel of AI hype is the lack of the right data. Despite lots of computing power and sophisticated data models. It's like driving a powerful sport car with no tires.

5
AUGMENTED REALITY
AND VIRTUAL REALITY

Augmented Reality

Pokemon Go is a perfect illustration of Augmented Reality (AR). Nintendo added a game figure that appears on a real time map on your smartphone. In order to 'catch' that figure, you have to physically walk to the specific place on the map. Then, using game controls, you can 'catch' that figure to collect more points. Thus, a new electronically generated entity was superimposed on a real map.

Another simple example of AR is the electronic visual trace of a golf ball's trajectory shown on a TV screen seconds after it was teed off. Without such visual traces, watching golf on TV would be much less appealing.

One of the neatest applications of AR is in retail when you want to try before you buy. You can upload a picture of your room and then try different virtual furniture in the context of your current room size and decor. Or you can pick a product and preview what it looks like in any room through your smartphone camera. Houzz Personalized Planning is a great example of that functionality.

Another is trying on different virtual make-up before you order the perfect one. All you do is upload a picture of your face and try different products before you spend a lot on cosmetics.

Augmented Reality is used on laptops, smartphones, tablets, and TV without needing special goggles. Industries most affected today include Entertainment, Military, and Architecture.

- Pokemon
- Electronic trace of a golf ball trajectory on TV screen
- Try before you buy - Houzz Personalized Planning
- Virtual makeup studio

Virtual Reality

Virtual Reality involves wearing special goggles and headphones that immerse the user in an electronic rendering of an environment that could be a reflection of the real world. A VR user feels like they're experiencing a simulated reality firsthand, mainly by vision and hearing.

Examples include simulated underwater exploration of a colorful reef based on 3D color pictures from multiple sophisticated cameras. Or it could be a complete fantasy world of a medieval castle full of Disney-like 3D figures floating around you.

The barrier for VR is the need to wear the large goggles. They are not practical when walking or driving. Thus, they are mainly used for sedentary applications at home—mostly games. Also, sharing these goggles among people has a hygiene aspect. How do you clean it between multiple users?

For a creative use of VR in business, please refer to an Architecture section. Like AR, VR has the most potential in Entertainment, Education, and Architecture.

VR also has interesting applications in specialized training, especially where there is a physical aspect to the mastery of a skill. For example, how would an MD connect a new medical device to another device, or attach it to a patient? Another example is providing VR instructions on how to remove or install parts in a complex vehicle. The training can be both passive–just watching—or active, where one needs to connect two objects in virtual reality, which is analogous to working on a flight simulator.

There are a lot of investment activities in this sector. In 2015, AR and VR start-ups raised over $650 million in equity financing.

- Special goggles
- Total visual and sound immersion

- Not practical to walk or drive in VR goggles
- A lot of investment activities in AR and VR

6
BIG DATA AND
DATA WAREHOUSING

Big Data denotes just.... more data.

The popular term *Big Data* was coined by META Group (now Gartner, an IT research company) to describe data sets that have:

1. High volume
2. High velocity
3. High variety

High volume means a lot of data in relation to what we used in the past (but META Group did not define how much data makes it 'big'); high velocity, which means high speed or real time data inputs and outputs; and variety, which refers to the range of data types (unstructured text and numeric from emails and posts, images, video, audio). Facebook data on 1.7 billion users would surely fit that definition.

Big Data is just a marketing term used to draw attention to the issues associated with the technical challenges related to the management of very large data sets that are quickly updated and contain various types of unstructured data.

In the not so distant past, most of the data to be analyzed was structured in rows and columns (think Excel) and did not change in real time (it was updated daily, weekly, or monthly). One exception is the high-speed transaction processing used by banks and large financial institutions; but even this doesn't meet the variety test.

Today, data also comes from emails, posts, comments, images, videos, and audio files, and it keeps changing non-stop in real time.

- Definition of 'Big' by Meta Group
  - o High volume
  - o High velocity - lots of updates in real time
  - o High variety - text, image, video, audio
- Marketing term
- Drawing attention to challenges of managing very large databases
- In the past, most data was just numbers in neat rows and columns

New business currency

The data, whether big or small, is the foundation of all business transactions and the *de facto* new business currency. It is the digital glue of the digital disruption, the digitization of existing processes, and the creation of new products and services. All these activities require a lot of data to work well. They also generate lots of data.

- New business currency
- Digital glue of digital revolution, which
- ...needs a lot of data and...
- ...generates a lot of data

Social media data

The best examples are social media platforms that are both data hungry and data intensive. Their success is based on the ability to collect as much relevant data as they can so they can sell it to advertisers. Their value is directly proportional to the number of users and their activities—hence data. Imagine the technical complexity of managing Facebook data generated by more than 1.7 billion users, constantly creating and sharing enormous amounts of new content globally.

Ecommerce data

Another example is an ecommerce site. To build an ecommerce site, we need product data, communication data, security data, and the room to store all future transaction data. Next we need customer data to design and implement a marketing campaign. Then we start collecting all the web traffic data, data on the behaviors of visitors and prospects on our website before they decided to buy, and then transaction data after the actual sale. Finally, we need fulfillment data, shipment data, and returns data, to name a few. Imagine the amount of data behind Amazon's ecommerce site, which sells 480 million different products.

IoT data

Internet of Things applications tend to create a lot of data as well. Imagine thousands of sensors residing on an oil platform sending measurement results to a central processor every millisecond.

Bigger is not always better

From the analytical perspective, the amount of data may be irrelevant to the process of discovery of patterns in the data. Actually, a lot of valid research can be done on a good sample of data.

We do not always need all of the data to draw statistically valid conclusions. Also, more data does not necessarily mean better data—especially if it is incorrect, irrelevant or incomplete.

However, we need all data when we want to summarize all transactions or do detailed reports broken down by various categories such as product, region, customer, etc.

- Bigger does not mean better
- Can do research on sample data
- Need all data for summaries and management reports

Data Warehouse, Data Mart, Data Lake

Data Warehouse is a term used to denote the functional scope and physical space where certain business data is stored. A Data Warehouse usually stores data belonging to a particular business department. Data Warehouse is just a marketing term applied to large business databases.

Conceptually, Big Data may reside in a Data Warehouse.

Companies would have a Sales Data Warehouse, a Financial Data Warehouse, or a Marketing Data Warehouse (or Mart or Lake) denoting the scope of their logical functionality.

'Marts' and 'Lakes' usually denote smaller databases, or logical subsets of larger entities. Thus, the Marketing Data Warehouse can be made up of a Social Media Data Mart (or Lake) and a Web Traffic Data Mart (or Lake).

If vendors continue along these lines of naming conventions, we may soon have Data Pools, Data Ponds, and Data Puddles :-)

From the technical and analytical perspective, these terms are completely irrelevant. Data analysis always included queries against databases, regardless how they are named, how they related to each other, or how big they were.

- Databases organized by business function
  - Sales Data Warehouse
  - Marketing Data Warehouse
  - Financial Data Warehouse

- Marketing Data Warehouse may be made up of
  - Social Media Data Mart
  - Web Traffic Data Mart
  - Online Advertising Data Mart

- From technical and analytical perspective, they are just databases

7
API
APPLICATION PROGRAMMING INTERFACE
A digital waiter

API is a technical term for a way to exchange data between various software applications on the Internet today.

For example, when you have a weather app on your smartphone, it does not store all the weather data on it—it just stores your location. When you want to check out the weather for today in your town, you click on a button. Behind the scenes, the button picks up your location and today's date. Then your smartphone sends your location and today's date to the central cloud-based database where all the weather data is stored for all days and all cities.

At the same time, the button passes the request to return the data only for your particular city and just for today. Based on that request, the central database returns a small file with the info on weather for your city today. After it reaches your smartphone, it gets formatted nicely to fit your screen—and voila!—in a few seconds you have info on the rain fall or sunshine coming soon to your town.

All software developers who work with apps and other Internet applications have already agreed to a standard way of passing that information back and forth between smartphones or browsers and the central databases. Just like we all agreed to drive on the right side of the road and have the gas and brake pedals in our cars next to each other with the accelerator being on the right side. To use another analogy, such a standard is equivalent to agreeing to speak the same language, thus avoiding the complexity of knowing many and having to translate from one to another.

Another useful analogy is to think about APIs in terms of eating out at a local restaurant. As a restaurant customer, you and your party pass the request for your food to the waiter, who accepts the order and in turn passes the request to the kitchen, which, after some time, returns the dish you ordered to you via the waiter. In any restaurant, there are many parties and customers, many waiters, many menu items, and one kitchen. They all speak English (or a local language) and hopefully you and your party get what you actually ordered in a reasonable timeframe and at the right temperature. The waiter is your API.

In a nutshell, this is all you need to know about APIs if you are not a programmer. One thing to keep in mind as a non-programmer is that any application your business develops may also benefit from accepting data requests via API. A good example here is providing managerial reports to your customers on the status of services you provide. Imagine that you manage a large apartment complex and you have all the data on all the requests for repairs from all the tenants, stored together with the status of repairs. You built that database to coordinate all repair jobs.

However, you can provide tenants with an additional benefit: a web page or phone app where they can check on the status of just their requests. This will reduce their anxieties and the number of phone calls to your employees.

A question to ask when evaluating any commercial software today is whether they support exchanging data via API. If they do not, look elsewhere.

8
BLOCKCHAIN
'Trust but verify' - Russian proverb

Imagine that every online transaction ever done by anyone, anytime, is stored in a secure database forever, tagged with a timestamp and the name of the person who entered it online. No one can hack it, and no one can delete it. It is 100% secure, forever, and easy to verify by anyone who was involved with it, as each transaction can be easily looked up anytime. No dictator or government agency can ever change it, and no drug or oil money can corrupt it.

For a moment, let's not worry about the technology involved. Let me just assure you that this is technically feasible today and already being used around the world on a limited basis.

By *transaction* I mean popular online activities such as:

- Paying a bill online
- Receiving a single invoice payment
- Sending/receiving money transfers to/from a family member

- Signing online contracts with e-signature
- Uploading a document
- Editing a contract
- Sending/receiving email

- Logging and reporting product shipment
- Logging and reporting product or material receipt

- Voting
- Responding to a survey
- Filling out a form requesting information
- Applying for jobs, permits, or memberships

- Downloading a song or a picture
- Clicking on an advertisement
- Viewing a video or a streamed movie

- Updating your health records by your doctor
- Filling prescriptions

Let's talk about the implications. The single largest one is enhanced **TRUST** based on **TRANSPARENCY**.

Do you really trust your bank 100% to not ever make a mistake transferring your money? Do you trust your bank to be 100% hack-proof, and that your identity will never be stolen? Few do.

Do you really trust that your documents (deeds, wills, contracts, agreements) will never be stolen, destroyed, or changed without your knowledge by omission or commission? Or your signature forged? Few do.

Do your really know where the products you buy come from and what they are really made of, and what health inspections they were subject to? Few do.

Do you really trust that all of our municipal, state, and federal votes or opinion polls were correctly and truthfully tabulated? Few do.

Do you think that artists today have a good idea who sold their songs, movies, and images and in what quantities, and how much royalties they should really receive? Few do.

Do you think that advertisers today really trust Google and Facebook with respect to the actual times an ad was displayed and clicked on? Few do.

Do you think that Google and Facebook have your privacy interests in mind? Few do.

Do you think that your medical records are safe in terms of privacy? Few do.

Do you think that your prescription drug purchase records are safe from hacking? Few do.

Do you think that tax agencies (federal and state) can trust the integrity of your tax returns? Do you think taxpayers trust federal and state tax agencies with respect to the right amount of taxes owed? Few do (as the rules are too numerous, hard to understand, and follow in most countries in the world).

Now imagine that in all the scenarios described above, all the involved parties can trust each other as they can easily verify all the transactions with a few clicks.

The known implications are **ENORMOUS,** but promise many more that are hard to imagine today.

If we were to implement blockchain technology across the board, the following things would happen:

- The majority of banks, tax auditors, tax preparers, tax attorneys, would not be needed and would cease to exist. So would federal, state, and municipal tax agencies. This would help to lower budget deficits and would result in an overall reduction in expenditures for governing—and could and should be passed to voters in the form of lower taxes. This would also result in a significant reduction in financial and legal fees, which could also be passed on to constituents.
- Elimination of money-laundering and severe reduction in systemic corruption. Fewer politicians will ever be tempted to abuse power. It would be almost impossible to hide such supplemental illicit income.
- Severe reduction in the number of lawyers working with contracts and litigating contract breaches. There would be no need for so many of them, as it would be very hard to breach the contract in the first place. The savings on lawyer fees will be passed on to customers.
- Less fraud, and thus a reduction in the number of lawyers, judges, prosecutors, and jail facilities. It would be much harder to defraud in the first place. The savings will be passed on to taxpayers and consumers.

-Increased quality of our food, with a simultaneous decrease in the price of food, as it will be easy to identify and eliminate dishonest suppliers and low-quality ingredients.

-More trust in civics, as voting fraud would be completely eliminated. More trust in the media, as poll reliability would increase. More voter engagement would follow as a result of less cynicism associated with the lack of governing transparency and less corruption.

-More effective advertising. Savings passed to consumers, not Google ☺.

-Better health records leading to better research and thus to better outcomes. Potential huge savings to the whole of society.

-More creative artists less frustrated with being ripped off, which equates to more inspiration for our souls.

In a nutshell, it is hard to overestimate the impact of more trust. One thing is certain; the use of technology enforces more accountability and transparency. This translates to trust. Trust translates to a lower cost of doing business, more social cohesion, more citizen participation, more creative expression, and more productivity, as rewards are more justly tied to outcomes. Isn't that what we are all really striving for?

I've presented here only a few tangible but tremendous benefits derived from recording, keeping, and protecting every online transaction; that is, trust. There are many more benefits that we may not be able to envision today. Just like it was hard for anyone to envision a portable camera combined with the portable phone (today called a smartphone) when Graham Bell presented his first phone in 1876, almost 40 years before the first 35mm camera was introduced in 1913.

A fundamental change like this is not going to happen overnight, as too many forces today have too much to lose from it. However, this is an inescapable trend loaded with a lot of great and optimistic possibilities. The question is not whether it will happen. It is already happening. The question is when it will happen on a large worldwide scale. And the sooner the better for the whole of humanity.

For your reference, here is Wikipedia's technical definition of a blockchain as a technology:

A **blockchain**[1][2][3] – originally **block chain**[4][5] – is a continuously growing list of records, called *blocks*, which are linked and secured using cryptography.[1][6] Each block typically contains a hash pointer as a link to a previous block,[6] a <u>timestamp</u> and transaction data.[7] By design, blockchains are inherently resistant to modification of the data. *Harvard Business Review* defines it as "an open, <u>distributed ledger</u> that can record transactions between two parties efficiently and in a verifiable and permanent way."[8] For use as a distributed ledger, a blockchain is typically managed by a <u>peer-to-peer</u> network collectively adhering to a protocol for validating new blocks. Once recorded, the data in any given block cannot be altered retroactively without the alteration of all subsequent blocks, which requires collusion of the network majority.

9
RFID
RADIO-FREQUENCY IDENTIFICATION

Here is the definition of RFID from Wikipedia:

"Radio-frequency identification (RFID) uses electromagnetic fields to a automatically identify and track tags attached to objects. The tags contain electronically stored information. Unlike a barcode, the tag need not be within the line of sight of the reader, so it may be embedded in the tracked object.

RFID tags are used in many industries; for example, an RFID tag attached to an automobile during production can be used to track its progress through the assembly line; RFID-tagged pharmaceuticals can be tracked through warehouses.

RFID tags can be attached to clothing and possessions, and implanted in animals and people.

In 2014, the world RFID market is worth US$8.89 billion, up from US$7.77 billion in 2013 and US$6.96 billion in 2012. This includes tags, readers, and software/services for RFID cards and labels.

A typical RFID tag will store unique tag serial number, and product-related information such as a stock number, lot or batch number, production date, or other specific information.

10
ANALYTICS

If you cannot measure you cannot manage

We define data analysis as the process of discovering useful information from data to support decision making. Like with many terms in the digital world, this one also overlaps with other frequently used terms such as statistics, data mining, data modeling, and data visualization.

Analytics = Data Analytics = Analysis = Data Analysis = Business Analytics = Business Analysis

Statistics vs. Analytic

If you think about statistics as a data science, think about data analytics as a practical application of data science in business decision making. Analytics is the application of statistics to real problem solving.

A good example of differences between statistics and business analytics is presented here:

Statistics : 30 +20 =50. In the abstract, this is just pure math: if you add 30 to 20 you get 50.

Analytics: If 30 represents the number of units of product A sold last year and 20 represents current year sales in units of the same product, then the more meaningful number is that our sales went down 10 units (30-20=10) or 33% since last year (10/30*100=33%), as compared to the fact that in two years we sold 50 units. Most managers would likely be concerned about a 33% drop in sales in one year as compared to total sales over two years.

- Statistics: 30+20=50
- Analytics: We sold 50 units in last 2 years but last year, sales went down 33%

Effective Analytics

Are these sales results good or bad or indifferent? This depends on a manager's goals and responsibilities. Maybe the plan was to sell 40 units in two years and now they are 10 units ahead of the game. Or maybe fewer units were sold the second year but at a much higher profit per unit? Or maybe the competition introduced a better product and even Zig Ziglar would not have been able to sell 30 units in the second year.

Was the manager's incentive bonus tied to units sold, or profitability, or market share? And so on and so forth…. Thus, business analysis is impossible to get right without an intimate knowledge of products, sales goals, market conditions, competitors actions, corporate politics, etc.

This is why meaningful business analysis cannot be left to scientists or statisticians focused on statistics and math only.

- Is it good or bad or indifferent?
    - Sales does not mean profit
    - What was the goal?
    - What was the competitive landscape?
    - What were the bonuses based on?

- Need to know very well:
    - Business context
    - Market
    - Products
    - Competition
    - Corporate goals
    - Corporate politics

- Analytics cannot be left to statisticians focused on math only

Required skills

Good analytical skills frequently go with good strategic thinking skills, knowledge of psychology and people, good product knowledge, and a causal mind (or the ability to diagnose a cause that may not be numerical but cultural and/or circumstantial). This is why many top CEOs are known for being very analytical—you need that skill (and some others) to lead any complex business.

A good business/data analyst in the 21st century needs to be effective on the continuum of skills from data collection, translating it to information, supplementing it with business knowledge, and finally, the wisdom to know how to apply digital technology to increase profits.

Good business data analysts are also usually creative problem solvers. The combination of their business knowledge with the knowledge of data and digital technologies makes them good candidates for designers of new digital products and services.

- Strategic thinking
- Knowledge of psychology and people
- Knowledge of digital technologies
- Causal mind - being able to diagnose a business cause
- Creative problem solving
-

Do you want to be a CEO?

A successful career as a business data analyst is a great stepping stone to the executive suite. A very good business analyst will most likely keep an eye on the corner office, hoping to become a Chief Digital Officer in the future.

Thus, if you are dreaming of an executive suite in a complex, 21st century business, start now by mastering business data analysis skills.

Good analytical skills are a stepping stone to:
- Digital product and services designers
- Chief Digital Officers
- CEOs

Analytics - Digital Gold Mine

The value of good data cannot be overestimated. It could mean the difference between life and death, or between bankruptcy and profitable growth.

Jet planes are the perfect example of data's impact on life and death decisions. Pilots fly combat jets by wire—they rely on instruments, or data, to make critical decisions. Wrong or missing data may mean flight termination. Good and early data detection of enemy aircraft may mean survival.

A big bank in Chicago, over 20 years ago, did not know the distribution of its own loan volume by industry and was not aware of the risk exposure when that industry experienced a serious downturn. It happened that a significant part of their lending portfolio was in that sector. This bank is no longer around.

In business, good data may be worth billions. Just ask Google and Facebook.

- Flying by wire
- Bankruptcy by ignorance
- Value of good business data

Analytics, Data Mining, Business Intelligence, Data Visualization, Executive Dashboards

Analytics, Data Mining, Business Intelligence, Data Visualization, Executive Dashboards, Decision Support Systems, and OLAP are all interchangeable marketing terms for using software to analyze data and come up with managerial reports, charts, and alerts. While jockeying for market positions, vendors come up with all these new terms, which causes a lot of confusion.

Today, all data analytics vendors provide 99% of the same functionalities. The differences between their systems are like the difference between Toyota and Honda. All of them do a decent job analyzing data.

The limit of analytics is not in the different functionality of tools from different vendors. They are all very similar. The limit of data analysis is in data relevance and quality as well as in the analytical skills of users. We will elaborate on this later in this section.

- Most analytical software has very similar functionality
- Limit is not in analytical software tools but in…
- …Data quality issues
- …Analytical skills

Analytics - Monitoring

These were three extreme examples to make a point. In most businesses, the impact of good, bad, or missing data is generally not that immediate or severe. After all, these businesses have functioned without perfect data so far.

Nevertheless, good granular data allows for the detailed monitoring of processes to increase efficiency and effectiveness. Monitoring is the first basic step. Without good data and analytics, we may have been flying by the seat of our pants, using gut feelings and experience, or just old fashioned guesstimating.

Just basic monitoring can bring a lot of value. We know who sold what and when to whom for how much and we get daily updates on variance from budget, so we are not surprised at month end that we did not meet the target.

In manufacturing, we know what machine produced what product, who worked on what shift, and the actual quantity and cost of inputs. In logistics we know what was shipped where, how long it took, and where all the trucks are at any given time. For monitoring, we need basic descriptive analytics such as minimum, maximum, mean, median, mode, and variance.

Good quality monitoring is required, but it's not a sufficient basis for the type of process automation that can lead to substantial savings in labor cost, for example.

- Monitoring as a first step
- No surprises
- Basic descriptive analytics
  - o Minimum
  - o Maximum
  - o Mean
  - o Median
  - o Variance
- Good monitoring can enable automation

After we collected all the data, translated it to information that enabled monitoring, and automated our processes, the next frontier was to optimize it.

Optimization

Manufacturing provides a lot of good examples of process optimization. It's one thing to know how much I produced and how much I spent. It's another thing to know whether I did the best job I could. Maybe too much energy was used, maybe a slight increase in the quality of input can greatly improve outcomes, maybe I should be cooling or heating the process sooner or later.

With the collection of relevant and sufficiently detailed data, we can answer these questions. We can not only monitor but also optimize the process.

For optimization, basic prescriptive statistics are not enough; we need to use sophisticated algorithms.

A good example of process optimization is soil irrigation. Water management is crucial in many parts of the world and even a 10% reduction in unnecessary usage can make a big difference.

Based on real time data about the type of soil, its moisture and temperature as well as ambient air temperature and humidity, and time of a day, a sprinkler turns itself on and dispenses the right amount of water, then shuts itself down.

The algorithm that is used calculates the minimum amount of water for the desired soil moisture, given factors that impact that moisture. In this case, ambient temperature and humidity impacts evaporation, which prevents a certain percentage of water from sinking into the ground.

- How much I did, how much I spent
- Did I do the best job with respect to:
    - Goals
    - Costs
    - Quality
    - Time constraints, etc
- Soil irrigation

Predictive Analytics

There are several sophisticated applications of real time analytics, especially when applied to real time, voluminous amounts of data. The fancy new term is Predictive Analytics. From the analytical perspective, it's just a lot of real time analytics based on an algorithm written by someone very familiar with the process.

This includes credit card fraud detection in the financial world, or predicting equipment failure.

In the case of credit card fraud detection, historical patterns of charges are compared with real life charges. If a customer has been charging 99% of their transactions over the last 2 years in stores with zip codes around their house and the highest single transaction did not exceed $2,000, then predictive analytics software will flag an attempt to charge $15,000 in an overseas store 8,000 miles away.

Another good example of predictive analytics is predicting equipment failure. One can do it by measuring an engine's vibration and/or input of energy. From previous analysis, it's known that a certain ratio or level of vibration to increased energy consumption indicates a mechanical problem with bearings.

When this ratio is measured in real time and exceeds the predefined level, software sends an alert (text, or email) flagging the need for service or replacement of critical equipment. The software can also send a signal to an automatic process controller to shut the whole operation down. Such logic is determined by the plant's operational managers.

- Credit card fraud detection
- Predicting equipment failure
- Automatic shutdown

The Achilles Heel of Analytics

The Achilles heel of business analytics is neither the amount of data we collect, nor the lack of statistical models or predictive algorithms.

Rather, it's related to these 3 phenomena:

1. Lack of relevant data (not collected at all and/or not granular enough)
2. Poor data integrity
3. Lack of compatibility

Lack of relevant data

If we do not collect sales data every 30 minutes by product, we will never be able to know how many burgers versus soups we sold between 11:30 AM and 12:00 PM. This may sound trivial, but collecting more frequent or more granular data costs time and money, and decisions need to be made as to the value of such a discovery.

Another example is our current weather prediction systems. We do not collect enough granular data about wind, temps, humidity, precipitation, etc. to be able to predict the weather in the next 24 hours with 99% certainty. To be that accurate, we would need to have many more weather stations installed and feed the data real time, but this is still too expensive. So we live with imperfection, as perfection is too expensive.

The last example is on data relevance. If you do not collect the data that drives things that you try to measure, you may never be able to explain what is going on.

Let's discuss the following simple scenario. You distribute several sunscreen products country wide through more than 2,000 retail stores. Your sales vary a lot by distributor and you have a hard time understanding that variation. You know that retail stores run their own promotions, but you do not know on which sunscreen type, when, and for what percent discount. In addition, you do not have weather data for all 2,000 locations, including outside temps and cloud coverage.

Common sense and experience tells you that sunscreen sales are driven by cloud coverage and local promotions. Thus, it becomes obvious that you will never be able to explain that variation in sales by retail store until you start collecting and analyzing data on the major drivers.

- If you do not collect, you cannot measure, thus you cannot manage
- Measurement granularity
  o Daily vs. hourly
  o Not enough data points
- Measurement relevance
  o Are you collecting data on real drivers?

o   Sun screen - no local promotion or weather data

Poor data quality

Many businesses today struggle with basic data integrity (missing, incorrect, duplicate, not timely). This is very typical when data is entered manually. As an example, customer names may be misspelled or appear multiple times, phone numbers and some sales dates are missing, addresses and gender representations are not collected. Therefore, it would be hard to come up with a simple correct analysis of sales by day, by gender, by city, and by household, for example.

There is no escape from the old adage— 'garbage in, garbage out'.

- Missing
- Incorrect
- Duplicate not timely
- Garbage in - garbage out

Data in silos

In today's global and competitive economy, one needs to be able to analyze data across multiple systems for conclusive profitability analysis, starting from a marketing campaign, through sales, production, distribution, and customer service. The lack of such information will prevent optimal pricing and resource allocation.

However, today, most marketing departments struggle to even understand the first step. Data from web traffic, email campaigns, online advertising, social media, and actual sales is in five separate systems that frequently don't 'talk' to each other. Therefore, we cannot determine which digital marketing channel is most effective and efficient, despite having all the detailed data paid for and stored on our systems.

This is a simple example of when the drivers are known, but the data is not collected. There is yet another problem, when the drivers are unknown but we have a hypothesis that needs to be verified. This is where sophisticated statistics would fit in, and this is out of the scope of our discussion.

- Imprecise picture of profitability by product, region, customer, etc.
- Departmental silos

Measurement Cost and Wisdom

"Not everything that can be counted counts, and not everything that counts can be counted." Unknown.

Measuring business activities is not without cost. Even if data storage cost is negligible, there is the cost of the technical staff's setting up systems to collect, cleanse, and organize the data, and then there is a cost of expensive knowledge workers to perform such analysis.

It is management's responsibility (with the input from data analysts) to decide what data needs to be collected and to determine that it's worth analyzing. As this quote says, 'Not everything that can be counted counts, and not everything that counts can be counted'.

We can count the number of grains of sand in a sandbox, but what is the point? And we cannot count friendship or loyalty, which count a lot.

Summary

- Crucial skill for 21st century executives

- Digitization means measuring more and better
- More measurement > More data collected
- Data is useless unless turned into information
- Information is useless unless it is supported by business knowledge
- Knowledge is useless if it is not wisely applied to make a profit

- Measurement leads to better monitoring
- Monitoring enables automation
- Automation enables optimization
- Optimization means higher profits

PART V
DIGITAL SKILLS GAP

1
DIGITAL SKILLS GAP DEFINED

Let's assume that we have solved issues related to data integrity, privacy, and security. As we've demonstrated, even the best management consulting firms are betting heavily on demand for assistance with digital transformation. The digital revolution is here—no one doubts it.

However....

...the most serious challenge to the success of the digital transformation is the lack of sufficient digital and analytical skills in the U.S. labor force.

Equivalent of a recession

According to McKinsey & Company, educational gaps like the digital skills gap, "impose on the United States the economic equivalent of a permanent national recession."

Burning Glass Technologies[3] found in 2015, that middle-skill jobs that require digital skills are outpacing those that do not. The study also revealed the following facts:

- 80% of middle-skill jobs require digital skills
- Digitally intensive jobs have grown 2.5 times faster
- Digitally intensive jobs pay 18% more

Lack of Digital Literacy

According to a Harris poll[5], almost 1 in 3 U.S. workers say they simply are not proficient in using the technology tools they need at work. What's more, only 1 in 10 American workers say they have mastered these tools.

From the same Harris poll: "Among workers we spoke to who use customer relationship management tools like Salesforce.com, 40 percent say they are not proficient with this technology. Over a third (35%) of workers using Hootsuite, a popular social media management tool, say they are not proficient at using it properly and only 11 percent consider themselves an expert."

According to IDC[5], "About 20 percent productivity loss occurs across the workforce due to factors including digital inefficiency. Our workforce is made up of nearly 160 million people, with about 84 percent – or 125 million people – working in information sectors with technology of some sort. This means that if the average annual wage of an American worker is around $50,000 and 20 percent of productivity is lost, businesses lose $10,000 in productivity for each worker. In total, it's a $1.3 trillion hit to U.S. businesses."

- 33% of U.S. workers are not digitally proficient
- Only 10% admit they have mastered the digital tools
- $1.3 trillion hit to U.S. businesses with GDP = $14 trillion

Managerial digital skills in short supply

In 2016, Bloomberg[4] asked 1,251 job recruiters at 547 companies about the skills they want but can't find while hunting for top MBA talent. The most desired and the least common were strategic thinking and communication skills. These are the crucial skills required to lead the digital transformation in any company.

Here is a very telling quote from Fast Company[6] supporting Bloomberg's findings above:

"More companies are requiring a mix of technology and people skills, and 2016 is being called the year of the hybrid job. In an analysis commissioned by Bentley University, researchers examined 24 million job listings, looking for key skills across nine industries. They found that employers want multifaceted employees who possess hard skills such as database technology, coupled with traditional soft skills like communication and collaboration....

Employers need staff that can compile, interpret, and apply data to their role and the company more broadly. Regardless of function, employees need to be able to effectively communicate what the data means and apply it to big-picture objectives, but this can't be done in a silo; collaboration and teamwork are essential. Not surprisingly, occupations pertaining to data analysis are the fastest growing today across multiple industries."

And the final remarks from the same (Bentley) 2016 study: "As more hybrid jobs are created, graduates and job seekers must commit to continuous learning to ensure their skill sets remain relevant, building new competencies based on market needs so they can prepare themselves for long-term career success. The best preparation for the changing job market begins in higher education and calls for a combination of professional courses with arts and sciences. This gives graduates a distinctive edge as employers today want candidates with practical, analytical skills embedded in a liberal arts education."

- Not enough MBAs with strategic thinking and communication skills
- Growing demand for hybrid jobs - mix of soft and digital skills
- Commitment to continuous learning

New jobs being born every day

The Future of Jobs, a new report from World Economic Forum[7] claims that 5 years from now, 35% of skills that are considered important in today's workforce will have changed. According to this report, "creativity will become one of the top three skills workers will need. With the avalanche of new products, new technologies and new ways of working, workers are going to have to become more creative in order to benefit from these changes."

- 5 years from now 35% of skills will have changed
- Creativity becomes 1 of top 3 skills

Skills gap across generations

The digital skills gap exists across generations. Millennials know some technologies, especially social media and smartphone apps, but lack analytical skills and experience with complex business processes. Baby boomers know business processes but may look to IT specialists for new technologies.

As large numbers of baby boomers are retiring and taking years of institutional knowledge and skills with them, transferring that knowledge will be very important to the successful digital transformation. Simply stated, you cannot digitize a process you do not understand... or come up with a new digital service without knowledge of consumer behaviors and preferences.

- Generational Digital Skills Gap
- Need to combine the knowledge of
  - o Technology
  - o Business processes

Types of digital skills

Digital skills could be grouped into 6 distinct clusters:

1. Computer programming/software design/database design - requires either a Computer Science degree or equivalent experience.
2. Hardware design - requires an Electrical Engineering degree.
3. Digital marketing - the knowledge of how to use software packages (but not to build them), and the knowledge of point-and-click interfaces are sufficient; but creativity and great communication skills are also required, together with the knowledge of business as well as excellent local language skills—both written and verbal.
4. Digitizing existing manual processes - requires knowledge of business processes and relevant technologies that may impact them. Good communication and change management skills are also very important.
5. Creation of new products in the context of Internet of Things (IoT) framework - requires knowledge of existing sensors, basic knowledge of various communication protocols with respect to their throughput and range, simple analytics and visualization of data, and good communication and business skills.

6. Data Analyst - requires skills along Data > Information > Knowledge > Wisdom continuum, supported by excellent communication skills, common sense, and business knowledge.

The first two groups require very specialized technical skills <u>and could be outsourced overseas.</u>

The remaining four blend different digital skills with creativity, communication, and business knowledge. We see the demand growing faster for the blended skill sets as compared to the highly technical. <u>The jobs in the last four groups are much less likely to be outsourced overseas.</u>

2
CLOSING THE DIGITAL SKILLS GAP

Students need to be inspired to see digital skills as a core skill – as fundamental as literacy and math. They need to be shown a clear path to how these digital skills translate to exciting and fulfilling careers.

They need to learn that 'digital' does not only mean complex computer programming or complicated computer network or database management. They need to learn how to <u>use</u> existing technologies, not necessarily how to build them—just like they need to learn how to drive a car to the desired destination on time and on budget, not how to build it.

- Digital Literacy and Numeracy
- How digital skills translate to fulfilling careers

- 'Digital' is not only computer science or electrical engineering
- It is also about how to use the existing tools
- It's not about building a car...
- ... it's about learning how to drive it...
- ... to the desired destination
- ... at the right cost and the right time

We strongly believe that such inspiring education should start in middle schools. It must go beyond the growing practice of providing tablets and network support to share courseware and resources. It's of paramount importance to teach, inspire, and prepare the next generation for what to expect from the digital reality waiting for them in the workplace.

"The mediocre teacher tells. The good teacher explains. The superior teacher demonstrates. The great teacher inspires." William Arthur Ward

- Start in middle schools
- Inspire and prepare the next generation
- Prepare for digital reality in their future jobs

Today, every professional job has as a digital component regardless of the industry. Using Excel, CRMs, social media, online search, emails, document management and sharing, basic graphics, or project management systems are daily routines. The smaller the company, the more versatility is desired of each employee. Thus, to graduate from high school we should require proficiency in the following skills:

- Excel, CRM, social media
- Online search, email campaigns
- Document management and sharing
- Basic graphics
- Project management

Inspirational digital curriculum - K-12

Such digital inspiration and education may involve:

- Introduction to the Digital Transformation framework
- Inspiration about the possibilities
- Proficiency in office productivity tools – word processor, spreadsheet, presentation, and email (either Office 365 or Google Suite)
- Hands-on digital workshops to build IoT apps
- Hands-on workshops to build smartphone apps
- Robotics labs
- Basic analytical skills with spreadsheets using business case studies
- Social media management
- Website development
- Graphical design
- Content Creation - Copywriting | Writing workshops
- Email marketing
- Security basics
- Network management basics
- Programming basics

- And many others...as demand changes

Such an inspiration could provide not only basic skills, but it could also guide students' vocational choices. They may get inspired by discovering various digital possibilities. Today, they may not even be aware of what's feasible.

- Vocational choices
- Inspiration about the possibilities
- Most are not aware of what is digitally feasible

Digital curriculum - college

We see a very similar approach to college education. Students may want to discover the Digital Transformation framework first. Such an introduction may inspire their course of studies. Most college students are not even aware of the plethora of exciting careers requiring digital skills.

In business colleges and graduate business schools, students can also be introduced to the exciting career of digital strategist. There is a growing demand for future business leaders with hybrid skills involving strategic thinking, digital, analytics, creativity, and personal communication.

- Similar approach to college students
- Future business leaders need to combine:
  - Strategic Thinking
  - Digital
  - Analytics
  - Communication
  - Creativity

Lifetime learning

In the realm of continuing education and professional development, we can see the never-ending need to keep digital skills fresh in an environment where technology changes are constant and overwhelming. From an entry level employee, all the way to the executive suite, everyone could benefit greatly from keeping up with technological changes. We all need to commit to a lifetime of digital learning.

For such a vision to materialize on an individual level, at least three things will have to happen:

1. Easy access to easily digestible knowledge about what is out there digitally, presented as instructional, motivational, and inspirational, especially for young students
2. Self-assessment of aptitudes in the context of that knowledge
3. Subsequent skills development based on such assessment

Ad 1. Online learning technologies offer a perfect engine to provide such education. Many examples of application of digital technologies are highly visual and lend themselves to videos. Subtitled videos could be supplemented downloadable scripts in PDF. A course can also include engaging quizzes (known as Gamification) as well as discussion boards to share common passions and interests to be moderated by a mature instructor.

The consumption of the content can be analyzed using statistics on participation, such as the number of views, time on task, test results, and participation in online forums. The composite results can be summarized for teachers and administrators in online effectiveness tracking dashboards (using the latest online analytical tools).

Ad 2. Not only are many students unaware of what is currently out there; they don't yet know what they are capable of in the context of their own skills, aptitudes, attitudes, personality, and interests. When I was a young teenager, I had no idea what I wanted to do and what I was good at. I was not alone. ☺

After we have inspired our students to consider the possibilities, it's time for a self assessment. This can be done using a reliable online self-assessment tool from highly acclaimed and well-established sources. The results can be confidential and/or easily shared with educators and/or future employers based on the student and/or parents preferences.

Ad 3. Ideally, after assessing skills, aptitudes, interests, and personality type, a student should expect to easily access online matching educational or vocational next steps or goals with a suggested path to achieve them.

On the other end of the spectrum, interested education providers or prospective employers could benefit from knowing so much about possible candidates. With the candidate's permission, while protecting their privacy, we could provide a great match between supply and demand.

And our matching quality should be much higher than the existing processes of comparing a few keywords between candidates' profiles and resumes with a vague program or job description.

The scenario described above is technically feasible. There are already many Learning Management Systems that can accommodate any curriculum. Skills assessments are already provided online. And all educational programs and jobs are posted somewhere on their respective websites or job boards.

The problem is that these three integral parts are not connected with each other today in an easy to use, friendly format. This reminds me of the problem of storing business data in separate silos that we already discussed in the chapter on Analytics and System Integration.

Thus, the solution calls for integration of existing elements and providing a dashboard view of it on a local level. By a local level, I mean a listing of all the available educational and vocational resources within the candidate's reasonable driving distance (with the exception of the online content).

3
ECONOMIC DEVELOPMENT IMPACT

So far we have discussed the digital skills gap on an individual level. However, if not effectively addressed, a digital skills gap will have a substantial adverse effect on competitiveness and thus the economic development of our cities, counties, regions, and states.

Attracting new businesses and retaining existing ones is directly tied to the current and future supply of a qualified labor force with the right digital skills. For any expanding business looking for a new location (or existing business looking for relocation), one of the major criteria for such an important decision is having the right skill set among the local population.

No single organization, be it a university, large corporation, school district, or training company can address the issue of regional workforce development by themselves. Closing the digital skills gap on a regional basis requires a lot of coordination on the part of the many players in the region.

We have already demonstrated how every job and every industry is impacted by the digital transformation. The future belongs to regions that will be the most effective in implementing high quality digital skills training programs across their key industries.

It is not only the training, though. On a community level, we will have to provide much better matching of educational, professional, employment, and other economic opportunities. Today, most of the matching happens with respect to traditional jobs based on rigid resumes and inflexible job and task descriptions. Future jobs will change faster than current job descriptions are being updated now!

We need to improve this inefficient process and also expand it to support aptitudes, talents, attitudes, apprenticeships, internships, entrepreneurship, and continuous education beyond K-12 and college.

New digital technologies, described in the previous chapter, can be highly relevant here by connecting all members of the community and facilitating seamless matching based on complex multidisciplinary criteria beyond simplistic and rigid job descriptions.

- Impact on regional competitiveness
- Workforce development
- Matching talents with local education
- Matching talents and education with local industry demands
- Matching students, teachers, schools, colleges, apprenticeships, entrepreneurships, nonprofits, and employers with each.

In the next part of this book we will discuss the major skills and employment issues and trends associated with the digital transformation. It is hard to predict the future, but there are certain trends that are pretty clear right now.

First, let's paraphrase a couple of relevant quotes from a famous American management guru, Peter Drucker:

'The only thing we know about the future is that it will be *(different)* digital.'

'The best way to predict the future is to *(create)* digitize it.'

These paraphrased quotes are spot on. There is no reason to believe that digitization efforts will be abandoned or even slowed down.

We know by now that digital technologies will only become less expensive and more powerful over time. We also know that there are still too many manual, processes that have an adverse effect on our productivity.

4
SKILLS AND JOBS OF THE 21ST CENTURY
Fads vs. reality

In general, there is a marked increase in the demand for people with digital skills such as copywriters, graphic designers, video producers, social media managers, online advertising specialists, and data analysts with great communication skills who can work effectively in teams.

Let's discuss the digital trends from two perspectives: consumer and business. We will start with consumer trends first. For each trend, we will identify the skills needed to succeed in that activity.

Social media

Social media took all of us by storm. Facebook has about 1.2 billion active users around the world and it completely disrupted traditional media.

Twitter, Instagram, Facebook, and LinkedIn are household names. Social media provide an invaluable service connecting families, friends, and business associates around the world in ways that were impossible just ten years ago. At the same time they carry tons of noise, trivia and banality, but that's largely the fault of the users and not the platforms.

If you are in politics or entertainment, run a B2C (business-to-consumer) enterprise, or you are an opinion leader, you ignore social media at your peril.

- Disruption of traditional media
- Electronic word of mouth

- o Politics
- o Entertainment
- o Opinion Leaders
- o B2C
- Skills
  - o Digital Marketing
    - Copywriters
    - Graphic designers
    - PR professionals
    - Online advertising
  - o Superior written
  - o Analytics

Smartphones

The decrease in hardware, software, and telecom costs has led to the proliferation of smartphones, which themselves are powerful computers with GPS capability. As mentioned earlier, in 2016, around the world, more people own smartphones than toothbrushes or toilets .

Smartphones originate over half of all Internet traffic and searches today. Over 65% of emails are being opened first on smartphones. We're just glued to these devices most of our days.

The smartphone boom is partially responsible for putting pressure on a lot of businesses to adjust to mobile technology on small screens and new possibilities related to GPS (to send a coupon during lunch time to all people near my restaurant, for example) as well as new payments and loyalty program methods. Local B2C (Business to Consumer) businesses are being forced to redo their websites, shift advertising from desktop to mobile, accept mobile payments, and roll out smartphone-based loyalty programs tied to their POS (Point of Sale) systems. This is a lot of work.

The importance of mobile presence and payments is demonstrated by these two examples:

• Home Depot announced in 2015 that it would spend $1.5 billion to improve its supply chain and other back-end systems related to mobile ordering. This is a lot of money to make sure that customers can buy things with just a few clicks on their phones.
• Another example is Hilton Worldwide, which is investing $550 million to serve its guests in their 'mobile moments' and transform its entire customer experience (18).

Mobile payments are already reality and I would expect that in five years they will be as popular as paying with credit cards now. Also, mobile cash is more secure than actual cash, which has a positive impact on small entrepreneurs in underdeveloped countries, especially. We expect that in five years, speech recognition software will be in everyday use.

- Everybody has one
- Increase in mobile advertising
- Mobile payments
- Speech recognition
- Skills
  - User graphical design
  - Mobile apps designer
  - Augmented Reality designer
  - Analytics
  - Hardware design

Customer Experience

The shift of power to customers has been brought about mainly by mobile social media. Customers can learn about, compare, discuss, and evaluate products and services anywhere, at any time, at no cost.

Retail customer expectations have been raised by the ease of use of smartphones, 1-click check-outs, and the ease of repetitive ordering (Amazon Dash Button), as well as friendly email notifications and reminders. Now customers expect a similar experience in all their digital interactions. This is probably the most impactful trend for the next five years.

A poor customer experience almost guarantees failure, but creating a good one could be very expensive. Just ask Home Depot, Disney, or Hilton Hotels. However as technologies become less expensive, the pressure will only grow for every organization to provide a seamless, hassle-free experience in all aspects of digital interaction.

Five-star type evaluation systems are here to stay and will expand to all products and services. Adopting a consistent rating system allows for quick comparisons and will put even more pressure on every business to manage their reputations more expeditiously.

- Customer is ROYALTY!

- Very high expectations
- Pressure on ease of use and hassle free in all digital interactions
- Multi-device support
- 5 Star Ratings
- Skills
  - Strategic thinking
  - Knowledge of business
  - Knowledge of customers
  - User Interface Design
  - Analytics
  - Software design

Speech recognition

Speech recognition is reaching 90-plus percent accuracy on leading platforms such as Amazon Alexa. Voice controls are very natural and highly desirable interfaces—if they work well. As voice recognition advances, it will complement traditional computer and phone inputs.

Other than obvious convenience, speech recognition is crucial for everyone whose hands should be free or functional—drivers, first responders, police, military, construction operators, and people with disabilities.

With better voice recognition, smartphones and social media will be used even more extensively as folks will be able to engage safely during long commutes in the privacy of their cars.

We can expect voice recognition to work with text-to-voice technologies to facilitate hands-off interaction with email, social media posts, and blogging.

- On all devices - not only smartphones
- Speech recognition and text to voice
- Translations
- Skills
  - Strategic thinking
  - User Interface Design
  - Analytics
  - Complex algorithms design

Skills required:
  - Strategic thinking

- o User Interface Design
- o Analytics
- o Complex algorithms design

Videos and Photography

The importance of videos and pictures will only grow. Like our voices, our vision is a perfect interface to the world. Videos are processed by our brains much faster than text or audio. Promotional materials with videos convert browsers to buyers much better than the alternatives. Until recently, video production and distribution was expensive, but the price points are falling quickly.

- Growing importance
- Lower cost
- Skills
    - o Photography
    - o Graphical design
    - o Video design and production
    - o Voice-overs
    - o Script writing
    - o Creativity
    - o User Interface Design

Skills required:
- o Photography
- o Graphical design
- o Video design and production
- o Voice-overs
- o Script writing
- o Creativity
- o User Interface Design

Virtual and Augmented Realities

Pokemon Go is a great example of using digital technologies in entertainment through games. People relax a lot when they can be actively engaged and absent from daily reality for a couple of hours. Virtual Reality goggles and Augmented Reality games are perfect technologies for engaging games.

Naturally, people like to form like-minded groups and compare themselves with each other. A fitness app is a perfect vehicle for that. You can set and track your goals while you are competing (in the cloud) with fitness aficionados around the world who you will never meet.

Between AR and VR, smartphones, and GPS, anything is possible. Game developers are so creative that there is no way to know what they will come up with next. If today we can play a virtual paintball game shooting each other virtually with our phones while running outside, it's hard to predict what might come next. And if we combine it with robots and some physical sensors, then the sky's the limit. Maybe one of the future games will transport us to the past to virtually change the DNA sequencing of our forefathers, so we can play Pokemon Go with our virtual ancestors from four generations back? Who knows.

- Growing importance
- Skills required:
  - Graphic Design
  - 3D design
  - Creativity
  - Analytics

Let's discuss how these digital trends relate to managing a business.

Cloud Computing

More cloud computing - Amazon and Microsoft cloud platforms make a very compelling case for putting all IT operations on Amazon Web Services (AWS) or MS Azure. Assuming top notch security and the right prices, any new business should have all computing in the cloud.

This is harder to achieve for mature businesses with a lot of legacy systems, but any new applications could be housed in the cloud. Amazon and Microsoft are not the only players in the cloud business, but they seem to have the most comprehensive solutions, including IoT support.

The federal government announced "Cloud First Initiative" in 2011 to cut waste and help agencies deliver services faster. The CIA chose Amazon's AWS in 2013. Approximately five million people use Microsoft Cloud for Government, which includes Office 365 and CRM Online Government. Government services are perfect to be housed in the cloud, as most of them do not involve any physical inventory.

There is one barrier to full adoption of cloud services. It is the potential for a vendor lock. IT executives do not want to be dependent on a single cloud vendor going forward. We agree this is not good business. Therefore, cloud service vendors will have to make it easy to switch between their services and support models so that an IT operation can be supported by two vendors in a seamless fashion.

With the current dominance of AWS, Azure, and Google, we can see just a few players controlling 90% of this market in a few years. This will be similar to the joint dominance of Microsoft Windows and Apple's operating systems on our desktop computers fifteen years ago. Or the current Google and Apple dominance of mobile operating systems where Android and iOS account for over 90% of the market. The more things change, the more they remain the same.

Microsoft's case for cloud computing is especially strong for companies who already use Microsoft products such as Office, Dynamic CRM and ERP, SQL databases, Business Intelligence tools, Skype, and Surface tablets.

Paradoxically, cloud computing will lead to fewer IT infrastructure jobs in the U.S. for two reasons. Due to specialization and economies of scale, there will fewer IT infrastructure workers needed per number of business employees, and these fewer experts can be found outside of the U.S.

- Growing importance
- Compelling case
  - o Lower cost
  - o Concentration on business instead of 'digital plumbing'
  - o Better security
- Vendor lock
- Paradox - fewer IT infrastructure jobs
- Skills
  - o IT Infrastructure management
    - Hardware procurement and maintenance
    - System software procurement and maintenance
    - Databases
    - Storage
    - Backup
    - Security, etc
  - o Complex contract management
  - o Analytics

http://fortune.com/2016/09/02/us-government-embraces-cloud/

Software development

The proliferation of less expensive but more powerful computers energized the software development community and unleashed a wave of creativity that has not yet subsided. What was unthinkable just a few years ago became not only possible, but it is very lucrative, too. Many young developers made fortunes developing iPhone apps by themselves. Creating mobile apps does not require heavy duty computer science skills, as many can be developed based on existing templates using vendor-supplied toolkits.

Other examples of creative software development include 3-D animation brought to us by Pixar, super realistic Virtual Reality (VR) games, streamed video services, such as Netflix, or the latest craze, Pokemon Go.

In business software, there are a lot of choices among many good and relatively inexpensive, cloud-based software options. They support the majority of popular processes from email marketing, social media management, content creation, CRMs, ERPs, accounting, and customer service.

Today, the bottleneck is not the lack of software or its cost, it is how quickly we can absorb all the progress built into different software packages.

- Graphical User Interface (GUI) design
- Systems analysis and design
- Knowledge of business
- Analytics

Skills:
- Graphical User Interface (GUI) design
- Systems analysis and design
- Knowledge of business
- Analytics

Cost of Knowledge Workers Is Growing

In many companies, the cost of professionals or knowledge workers is the single largest ongoing and growing expense. Professionals are also their best assets. Increasing their productivity is of the greatest importance. Well-designed software may have a fundamental impact on the productivity of knowledge workers. Imagine financial or marketing analysis without an electronic spreadsheet, a sales rep without a smartphone phone and email, or a search without Google.

At the end of the day, good software serves only one purpose: to do the same task in less time. Implementing good software is a must if a company wants to increase the productivity of its most expensive assets— knowledge workers.

- Single largest expense
- Increase in productivity via superior software

Division of labor - specialization

The division of labor will only intensify due to the increasing need for specialization. Businesses will partner with digital marketing agencies and IoT providers. Most companies, especially smaller ones, would not be able to hire and retain the right talent; they need to find a reliable digital partner.

Division of labor is also being manifested in outsourcing 'digital plumbing' to cloud computing providers. As mentioned earlier, this trend will accelerate in the coming years.

- Business and Digital Marketing Agencies
- Business and IoT providers
- Business and cloud services providers
- Skills
  - Superior communication
    - Written
    - Verbal

Chief Digital Officer

The Chief Digital Officer has become a standard position in the executive suite. The number of CDOs has doubled from 2013 to 2014 and is expected to double again in 2015(11). CDOs are charged with coordinating and managing digital transformation, including building out entirely new businesses. They report to CEOs. Here is a quote from a McKinsey article:

"Getting the strategy right requires the CDO to work closely with the CEO, the chief information officer (CIO), business-unit leaders, and the chief financial officer; the CDO also needs to be an active participant in and shaper of the strategy. An important foundation for CDOs to establish credibility and secure a seat at the strategy table is providing detailed analysis of market trends and developments in technology and customer behavior, both inside and outside the sector".

- As 'digital plumbing' gets outsourced...
- ... more focus on leveraging digitization in business
- Skills
  - Digital Technologies
  - Strategic Thinking
  - Causal Thinking
  - Creativity
  - Analytics
  - Superior communication
    - Written
    - Verbal

Blurring lines between Marketing And IT

Moreover, the lines are blurring between Marketing & IT. It will become harder and harder to distinguish what belongs to marketing and what belongs to the Information Technology department. For example, a smartphone app for members of an exclusive country club allowing them to order meals or valet services ahead of time perfectly blends marketing and IT.

The app was built to improve customer retention, a marketing goal, by a team of marketing and IT folks collaborating on this task. The new service was feasible only because of the wide availability of smartphones and it was initiated by the marketing staff. Is it a marketing or IT project? It's really both.

- Related to Chief Digital Officer trend
- Marketing is dependent on IT
- IT is dependent on Marketing
- Skills
  - Digital Marketing
  - Business Software
  - Teamwork
  - Communication
  - Creativity
  - Analytics

The very rapid decrease in hardware, software, and telecommunication costs has enabled the collection, movement, storage, and real time analysis of massive amounts of data. This enabled business models where the service is free and the cost of running the service is covered by digital advertising (Facebook, Google to name a few).

This is how digital advertising was born…Actually, advertisers paid the lion's share of costs related to the digital revolution. We are sometimes annoyed with advertising online, but let's not forget their contribution to the technological revolution. They bankrolled a big part of it!

Online advertising will grow due to the very high precision and low cost of digital advertising as compared to traditional methods. Reaching 2,000 prospects in a printed magazine may cost $500 compared with $75 when using social media.

In addition, online ads have higher conversion rates, meaning that more people who see an ad do something about it because it's very easy to click and engage (as opposed to a magazine, where you need to call or get to your computer to order or learn more).

Nevertheless, the quality of advertising has to change. Between 2014 and 2015 the number of people worldwide who installed ad-blocking software on their mobile phones has doubled to 440 million. Over 80% of users mute video ads. People are just annoyed with the aggressiveness and inconvenience of ads that obstruct the content they want to read or watch.

Imagine if all ads were to be blocked tomorrow. Google and Facebook, among others, would go out of business immediately, or they would have to start charging for their services….

….actually Google already does: YouTube charges $10 a month for content with no ads. This may become the future model—if you don't want ads but want the content, you need to pay a subscription fee.

- Growing demand for good mobile ads
- Much less expensive – more effective
- Poor quality of advertising threatens the business model
- Skills
    - Digital Marketing
    - Creativity
    - Copywriting
    - Graphic design

- o Superior communication
- o Analytics

Skills required:
- o Digital Marketing
- o Creativity
- o Copywriting
- o Graphic design
- o Superior communication
- o Analytics

Speaking of analytics…In the real estate business, it's location, location, location. In the digital world, it's analytics, analytics, analytics.

We bring up this segment as the last one in our discussion about major digital trends. This is because it is one of the most consequential and significant digital skills one can master.

The paradox of today's digital world is that we collect much more data than we utilize. Data collection costs time and money. If collected data is not used, that investment is wasted. To add insult to injury, by not using collected data, we may forgo the discovery of warning signs or a great opportunity. So it's a double waste.

On the other hand, the timely discovery of risks and opportunities may save a business from bankruptcy or assure profitability. We've already discussed the bank in Chicago that was blindsided by the lack of knowledge of its own customers' problems. This led to the bank's total demise.

On a positive note, if we can identify an upward sales trend of a very profitable product in one region early in the year, we may want to order, manufacture, or distribute much more of this product to similar regions (or a whole country, or the whole world, assuming the same competitive landscape) to grab market share and register record profits.

In the past, a lot of successful companies were built without complex analytics. A lot of decisions were made on experience, trial and error, flying by the seat of our pants, or guesstimating. This was fine as long as the competition was employing the same low tech techniques. The business world was much less competitive and less complex.

Now, with growing global competition and larger, more complex operations, good analytics can make the difference between success and failure. Our earlier analogy of a jet fighter pilot flying by wire is relevant here. Yes, a pilot can be very experienced in flying, but it is impossible to pilot a combat jet on just human senses. One needs to react to instruments interpreting real time data feeds coming from many sensors placed on neuralgic jet components. Flying by the seat of our pants is not an option on an F-16.

Neither is it in robotic surgery on eye hernias, running complex manufacturing and supply chain processes, or optimizing the electric power grid.

- More measurement, more data, more analytics
- More intense global competition
- Single most important skill in the 21st century complex business
- Stepping stone to executive suite
- Skills
  - Strategic Thinking
  - Digital Technologies
  - Causal Thinking
  - Creativity
  - Analytics
  - Superior communication
    - Written
    - Verbal

Digital Collar Jobs

A lot has been discussed and written about the future of white collar jobs as they may get replaced by robots, artificial intelligence, and overseas contractors, among others.

A lot has been discussed and written about the demise of blue collar jobs lost to automation, international competition, and technological innovations.

Nevertheless, I see the emergence of hybrid jobs that require a blend of blue collar trade skills with white collar skills, such as problem-solving and digital proficiency. Let's call them digital collar jobs.

Digital collar jobs will never get outsourced overseas, or be replaced by robots. Nevertheless, they will always be enabled by the latest digital technologies.

The premise of the Internet of Things is that 'all things' will be connected to the Internet. Most of these 'things' will be sensors allowing the detection of movement, temperature changes, weather conditions, light intensity, presence of chemicals, pressure, electric currents, etc. Another category of 'things' will be distributed meters to remotely calculate electricity usage, flow of liquids (e.g., drinking water and sewage), compressed air, or any other consumables used in service and manufacturing processes. The third category of 'things' includes GPS devices, cameras, drones, and connected cars.

To install, calibrate, service, and maintain billions of these devices will take an army of digital collar workers. They will have to be able to do physical installations of these 'things' in many challenging places (attics, highway overpasses, skyscraper rooftops, basements, etc). At the same time, they will need to have digital skills to install, trouble shoot, diagnose, connect, and calibrate these devices. In many instances, it will require good communication skills for effective troubleshooting supported by remote technical help desks, online chats, and digital libraries.

The best example is the need to install, service, and calibrate the cameras, sensors, drones, and telecommunication devices needed to optimize traffic in all of our cities. Another example is the installation and maintenance of all sensors and devices to make our existing buildings smart enough to optimize energy usage for heating, AC, and lightning. And last but not least is the demand for the installation of sensing devices in construction and manufacturing processes as well as telemedicine applications; someone will have to install, service and connect a multitude of future remote medical diagnostic equipment and make sure that the results are protected for privacy.

In addition, local service jobs will have a digital component such as smartphone and GPS supported dispatch, job and materials tracking, and timeliness and customer satisfaction tracking. Digital collar workers will have to be comfortable with these tracking and reporting technologies, regardless of whether they are employees, employers, or managers.

As new generations of more capable sensors, cameras, devices, and telecommunication gear become available, there will be a need to replace the old generation equipment.

Since digital technology progress is not going to slow down anytime soon, there will be a steady demand for these services as well as a steady demand for keeping up with the digital skills to install and service them.

You don't need a college degree to be very good at these digital collar jobs. In addition, I can see a lot of opportunities for entrepreneurship in a digital collar installation and maintenance business that contracts with producers of these devices. Finally, these jobs, or self-employment ventures, do not preclude the pursuit of a college degree if it is in the interest of a digital collar professional in the future.

As discussed earlier, digital collar jobs will always be local and will never get outsourced or replaced by technologies. But they will be enabled by digital technologies—hence knowledge of these technologies is of paramount importance.

To make digital collar jobs and careers a reality, we need to rethink how and what is being taught in K-12 schools. We also need to think how we can support creative apprenticeship and entrepreneurship programs that do not require college degrees. Today, 70 percent of high school graduates do not go to college, but many are eager to get good jobs or start their own businesses. By the way, any future digital collar business owner will also need proficiency in digital marketing and social media to promote their businesses online.

Thus, with well thought out digital education programs, we can build a foundation for the best of three worlds as far as workforce development is concerned. The same program can support future digital collar jobs and future digital collar businesses, and keep the road to college open if so desired.

These digital collar careers will always be interesting—unlike some traditional blue collar jobs—as digital collar workers will need to keep up with constantly changing technologies. And with the proliferation of billions of connected 'things', I see a growing demand for the skills needed to keep all of these 'things' installed, calibrated, diagnosed, serviced, and replenished every couple of years.

CONCLUSION

Yogi Berra got it right. "It's déjà vu all over again."

Since the 1900s, when almost 40% of the U.S. population worked in agriculture, we have arrived in the 21st century with only 2% of the labor force working on farms.

In the meantime, we have invented or commercialized electricity at home, cars, airplanes, radio, TV, phones, satellites, computers, air conditioning, life saving antibiotics and vaccines, plastic surgery, and yoga instructors. All of them were hard to imagine for most contemporaries just before these inventions materialized. All of them were considered luxuries at the time. Now, they are necessities.

At the same time, we have increased wealth in the U.S. by a factor of about 8. So, on average, we are all 8 times richer than we were about 100 years ago based on a 2% annual compounded growth rate.

How did we accomplish such tremendous success? The answer is very simple: we have been increasing productivity per person through massive automation. Automation that was driven by our creativity to pursue happiness and personal freedoms by way of making more money for ourselves, our families, and our communities.

Thus, the more things change the more they remain the same.

The future is bright

We should welcome the digital transformation. It is a continuation of the trend that started even before the 1900s. It is not going to eliminate work and replace us with robots. On the contrary, it will make our jobs more rewarding by automating mundane, boring, error prone, hard, heavy, dangerous, dirty, and smelly tasks, and let us do more of what we enjoy and what we are good at.

It will improve our productivity even further, thus allowing for more luxuries (which, in 50 years, will become necessities). I suspect that in 20 to 30 years, **most** of us will have partial ownership in a private jet and the check-in line at airports will be a forgotten nightmare.

We will travel extensively worldwide, staying in even more luxurious resorts and taking more fancy cruises. We'll have much larger homes, and enjoy much more luxurious cars that will even drive themselves. We will have much more—and more luxurious—clothing. Everyone will have several luxury watches. Our food choices will be even more plentiful (if you can imagine that). The food will be healthy, fresh, and flown in from all over the world with a voice command whispered into a smartphone.

Our political process will be more transparent and accountable, based on social media scrutiny and higher voter engagement. It will be facilitated by easier communication and the millennials' frustration with the current lax political transparency. We may even pay off our national debt!

We will live longer with a better quality of life due to medical improvements. Most of us will have at least one plastic surgery to look younger and more attractive. A lot of us will have personal assistants, coaches, yoga instructors, and shrinks.

We will enjoy more arts and live entertainment by flying across the world to see a favorite band playing live. In a nutshell, more of us will have the lifestyle of today's well-to-dos, and today's well-to-dos will move into the super-rich bucket.

When not enjoying luxuries, we would spend much more time learning on an ongoing basis. Actually, it is my prediction that the only distinction between winners and losers will be the amount of time they spend continuously educating themselves.

This does not mean that the losers will be poor economically – they will have more affluence than today's middle class. They will just enjoy less social respect, as avoiding continuous learning will be socially frowned upon like smoking or obesity are now.

I predict that our tax structure will provide heavy incentives for learners and provide options to write off the cost of continuous learning for all.

This does not mean that some folks will not be affected by job losses and/or the need to retool in mid-career, or even several times during their active professional lives. Actually, changing careers many times during a lifetime will be the new norm. Thus, it's even more important that we should provide superior inspiration, training, and opportunity matching capabilities to today's youth.

Hard work ahead

This rosy picture does not assume a lack of effort, hard work, thinking, and education. On the contrary—to take full advantage of future opportunities and thrive in the 21st century, we will have to double or quadruple down on the amount and quality of available education. We will also have to significantly improve the matching of talents with resources on the local level.

It will strengthen our local communities by giving them a greater feeling of independent accomplishment. It will bring folks closer together by better communication and coordination of support for specific local needs.

It is worth noting that 70% of the U.S. population has no college degree. This is similar to most developed countries. But even a college degree is not enough for one to thrive in the 21st century.

Actually, the future belongs to individuals who, regardless of their official educational attainment, will treat learning as a key lifetime activity. Such an attitude toward education will allow people to continually reassess their own aptitudes and skills in the context of never-ending change.

The future belongs to accountable businesses and transparent processes. Blockchain technology combined with an increased standard of customer experience will reward ethics and civility even more.

This is also nothing new, just an acceleration of existing trends. Commercial activities have always contributed to more civility, as commerce trumps conflict.

I remember how shocked I was about how nice and trustworthy Americans were when I first came to the United States many years ago. Back in the drab times of communism, everyone back in the old country was very rude to each other. The level of trust was near zero.

When I went to visit my native Poland after 20 years' absence, I was shocked again, this time how much nicer people had become to each other in my homeland. What happened? McDonalds and other Western businesses expanded there after the fall of communism. They brought with them a strange idea of service with a smile (today referred to as the customer experience). This high level of customer service has trickled down to other businesses…and subsequently to society as a whole.

Skills you can bet on

We will always need doctors, teachers, plumbers, chefs, artists, nurses, scientists, managers, and sales people, among others. They will never be replaced by AI-driven robots. On the contrary, their jobs will be enhanced with digital technologies helping them to be better doctors, teachers, plumbers, etc.

As far as new types of jobs spun by the digital transformation, we discussed some of them in the previous chapter. However, it is hard to predict all the future job categories as they will keep changing over time.

But it is not hard to predict what skills will make you a winner. My prediction is that **the future belongs to creative analytical interdisciplinarians.**

Sam Walton was one of them. If he were alive today, he would be worth more than Bill Gates or Jeff Bezos by a factor of 2 or 3.

What he did was classic; he quickly recognized the potential and applied emerging digital technologies to the unglamorous business of a discount department store. He was creative, analytical, and interdisciplinary. He saw the potential of technology in the automation of processes such as shipments, payments, reordering, etc.

While Sears executives were congratulating themselves on their own brilliance, Sam Walton worked hard to connect all his stores with the latest and greatest computer communication equipment to <u>automate and optimize</u> his supply chain. Sears is no longer a viable business, but Walmart is the single largest U.S. employer with 1.5 million associates working there. And Sam Walton started Walmart by himself with a single store in the middle of Arkansas while Sears was at the peak of their glory.

I see the future full of opportunities for creative, analytical minds spanning various disciplines that are today taught in separate academic departments. Case in point is modern marketing where one needs to draw on the knowledge of computer science (e-commerce website building), arts (graphic design), statistics (conversion analytics), business (financials) and education (to educate and engage customers).

As the complexity of the world is not going to lessen, an analytical, creative, critical thinking mind will be at premium. The cost of the wrong decision will only grow and, conversely, a good decision may be priceless.

The last but rarely discussed ingredient of success in the 21st century is the right attitude. One will accomplish nothing of significance with arrogance, poor communication skills, cynicism, or a sense of entitlement. Why? Because, more than ever, due to multiple parties being involved in almost anything we do, superior communication, and thus motivational skills, are a must. They are just not compatible with the wrong attitude. Few have ever bought much from anyone with a bad attitude (unless their life depended on it).

Learn, learn, learn…

In summary, to thrive in the 21st century, learn as much as you can from various disciplines and talk or meet with as many people from all walks of life as you can. Travel as much as you can afford, especially to less fortunate countries or even neighborhoods. This will build your knowledge base, provide a healthy perspective, and stimulate your problem solving creativity.

The history of science

Learn the history of science. Science teaches critical thinking, experimentation, and analytics—all crucial 21st century skills. It does not mean you have to major in science; but learning the history of science would enhance your analytical skills a lot. Most scientists have very analytical minds as their job is to find out how things work either in biology, chemistry, physics, or any other discipline. Why not learn from the best?

Human history

Human history, on the other hand, will teach you that, very likely, the problem at hand—either personal, or societal, or political, or economic, or even scientific—has probably been experienced and solved, or at least addressed, and discussed by others before.

This will save you a lot of frustration and can generate useful ideas on how to leverage such experiences in current circumstances. After all, as humans, we have not changed much in the last 5,000 years since we have written records. We still make decisions emotionally but justify them with reason...

Most problems in life are not technical. Most problems faced by humans are based in relations with other humans. This will give you a good background in problem solving—a crucial skill for the 21st century.

In addition, take critical thinking classes and observe or participate in debates. They are a very good training ground to understand that you will never be able to win all arguments, or convince all voters, or sell all prospective customers. But you can learn to win, convince or sell *some*.

Your favorite technology

As far as technology goes, you can learn a lot on your own by tapping into some of the many free online resources, including free subscriptions to specialized blogs by industry thought leaders. In addition, you can join local meet-ups where people discuss in person the technology you are interested in. You can practice your interpersonal skills there as well.

Given the very rapid changes in technologies, it will be hard to find up-to-date curriculum delivered via traditional methods such as printed books and lectures. Be proactive in learning technology on your own from any reasonable and reputable online source.

Professional writing

Take a lot of writing courses and at least one technical writing class. After all, the Internet is built on matching text, not videos or images. Writing is not going away anytime soon. Please note that even if you want to concentrate on videos or movie making, someone will have to write a script, screenplay, or even a proposal to get your venture funded. If you want to start a music band, someone will have to write lyrics.

Professional speaking

Last but not least, practice public speaking as much as you can. Why? Most likely you will be working with many professionals of various backgrounds at the same time. This is due to the specializations forced by the sheer amount of knowledge.

Thus, your effectiveness will be tied directly to your ability to convey your ideas and win people over based on your eloquence. You can have an IQ of 180, but if you cannot speak and write in a clear and appealing style, your options will be severely limited. Your future income will be tied more to the quality of your communication than to your professional expertise.

Expertise is necessary, but it's not sufficient on its own to insure success.

Assess your talents

Assess your talents with reputable specialized assessment tools. The main objective of taking a self-assessment is to understand what you are good at and what you may enjoying doing in the context of future possibilities.

This will save you a lot of the time and frustration associated with a random and time-consuming self-discovery that may take years. Based on the assessment results, devise a plan to acquire the knowledge and skills needed to achieve your goals.

Final thoughts

You may be wondering why the final chapter talks so little about various technologies while this book is devoted to the digital transformation.

The answer is very simple. Technologies will change and there is no way to predict when and how. All we know is that they will change soon and fundamentally. The pace of technological change is not going to slow down anytime soon. Even if you concentrate on a particular technology today, it is unlikely that you will be working with it for the rest of your professional life. You will be using many different ones and some that are maybe even hard to envision today.

The only constant in our ever changing world are the principles of learning, analyzing, ethics, and communication. You will be able to work with any technology of your choosing, even inventing new ones. However, to reach your full potential, you will have to think, create, and work transparently with large groups of professionals spread around the world.

Technology is only the tool. As powerful as it is, it's just a tool. We need to know what we want to do before selecting the tools to do it.

It seems to me that most of us want to pursue happiness while improving our wealth, health, and civics.

INSPIRATIONS

Computers are incredibly fast, accurate, and stupid; humans are incredibly slow, inaccurate and brilliant; together they are powerful beyond imagination. *Unknown*

Ability is what you're capable of doing. Motivation determines what you do. Attitude determines how well you do it. *Lou Holtz*

Virtually nothing is impossible in this world if you just put your mind to it and maintain a positive attitude. *Lou Holtz*

Your attitude, not your aptitude, will determine your altitude. *Zig Ziglar*

We must accept finite disappointment, but never lose infinite hope. *Martin Luther King, Jr.*

Attitude is a little thing that makes a big difference. *Winston Churchill*

Success is no accident. It is hard work, perseverance, learning, studying, sacrifice and most of all, love of what you are doing or learning to do. *Pele*

Live as if you were to die tomorrow. Learn as if you were to live forever. *Mahatma Gandhi*

You must be the change you wish to see in the world. *Mahatma Gandhi*

If you don't like something, change it. If you can't change it, change your attitude. *Maya Angelou*

Without change there is no innovation, creativity, or incentive for improvement. Those who initiate change will have a better opportunity to manage the change that is inevitable. *William Pollard*

Times and conditions change so rapidly that we must keep our aim constantly focused on the future. *Walt Disney*

Change is the end result of all true learning. *Leo Buscaglia*

The business of America is business. *Calvin Coolidge*

Without economic development, any potential for political openness and freedom will be questionable. *Jose Maria Aznar*

Political freedom cannot exist without economic freedom; a free mind and a free market are corollaries. *Ayn Rand*

Millions of individuals making their own decisions in the marketplace will always allocate resources better than any centralized government planning process. *Ronald Reagan*

It's the economy, stupid! *James Carville, Bill Clinton's Lead Strategist*

It's the digital economy, stupid! *Unknown*

Think globally, source locally. *Unknown*

If you think education is expensive, try ignorance - *Derek Bok, the former president of Harvard University*

It's the education, stupid! *Unknown*

An investment in knowledge pays the best interest. *Benjamin Franklin*

We only think when we are confronted with problems. *John Dewey*

The roots of education are bitter, but the fruit is sweet. *Aristotle*

The principle goal of education in the schools should be creating men and women who are capable of doing new things, not simply repeating what other generations have done. *Jean Piaget*

Our scientific power has outrun our spiritual power. We have guided missiles and misguided men. *Martin Luther King, Jr.*

A good teacher can inspire hope, ignite the imagination, and instill a love of learning. *Brad Henry*

It is the supreme art of the teacher to awaken joy in creative expression and knowledge. *Albert Einstein*

The mediocre teacher tells. The good teacher explains. The superior teacher demonstrates. The great teacher inspires. *William Arthur Ward*

The art of teaching is the art of assisting discovery. *Mark Van Doren*

Ignorance, the root and stem of all evil. *Plato*

If a man neglects education, he walks lame to the end of his life. *Plato*

Knowledge becomes evil if the aim be not virtuous. *Plato*

The educated differ from the uneducated as much as the living from the dead. *Aristotle*

Education is the best provision for old age. *Aristotle*

Wisdom begins in wonder. *Socrates*

Teaching is the highest form of understanding. *Aristotle*

GREG GUTKOWSKI

Those that know do. Those that understand teach. *Aristotle*

Educating the mind without educating the heart is no education at all.
Aristotle
The cure for boredom is curiosity. There is no cure for curiosity. *Ellen Parr*

ABOUT THE AUTHOR

Greg Gutkowski, Digital Strategist & Bestselling Author has over 20 years of multidisciplinary global business experience spanning marketing, sales, and IT management, as well as Internet software development, IoT, advanced data analytics, and journalism. Greg has earned the following advanced degrees: MBA in IT Management, MS in Economics, MS in Journalism.

He currently runs the business analytics software company 3CLICKS.US and teaches digital strategies at the University of North Florida Coggin College of Business.

Greg has worked over the years with customers from various industries. He has helped, among others: Allstate, American Express, Aon/Hewitt, AT Kearney, AT&T, Blue Cross Blue Shield of Illinois, Charmer-Sunbelt, Continental Bank, Dean Foods, Exxon-Mobil, First Bank, John Alden Life, Ralph Polo, United Stationers, and University of North Florida.

He has also designed analytics systems for several K-12 public and private school districts across the U.S. to assist them in evaluating the effectiveness of various education programs. His analytic software have been implemented by many leading U.S. school districts.

Connect with Greg on LinkedIn at
https://www.linkedin.com/in/greggutkowski